Technical Briefing

Making Multiple-Objective Decisions

Mansooreh Mollaghasemi
Julia Pet-Edwards

IEEE Computer Society Press
Los Alamitos, California

Washington • Brussels • Tokyo

Library of Congress Cataloging-in-Publication Data

Mollaghasemi, Mansooreh.
 Technical briefing: making multiple-objective decisions /
Mansooreh Mollaghasemi, Julia Pet-Edwards.
  p.   cm.
 Includes bibliographical references.
 ISBN 0-8186-7407-5
 1. Multiple criteria decision making.   I. Pet-Edwards, Julia.
II. Title.
T57.M6   1997
658.4 ' 03—dc21   96-45233
                                   CIP

IEEE Computer Society Press
10662 Los Vaqueros Circle
P.O. Box 3014
Los Alamitos, CA 90720-1264

IEEE Computer Society Press Order Number BR07407
Library of Congress Number 96-45233
ISBN 0-8186-7407-5

Additional copies may be ordered from:

IEEE Computer Society Press	IEEE Service Center	IEEE Computer Society	IEEE Computer Society
Customer Service Center	445 Hoes Lane	13, avenue de l'Aquilon	Ooshima Building
10662 Los Vaqueros Circle	P.O. Box 1331	B-1200 Brussels	2-19-1 Minami-Aoyama
P.O. Box 3014	Piscataway, NJ 08855-1331	BELGIUM	Minato-ku, Tokyo 107
Los Alamitos, CA 90720-1264	Tel: +1-908-981-1393	Tel: +32-2-770-2198	JAPAN
Tel: +1-714-821-8380	Fax: +1-908-981-9667	Fax: +32-2-770-8505	Tel: +81-3-3408-3118
Fax: +1-714-821-4641	mis.custserv@computer.org	euro.ofc@computer.org	Fax: +81-3-3408-3553
Email: cs.books@computer.org			tokyo.ofc@computer.org

Publisher: Matt Loeb
Acquisitions Editor: Bill Sanders
Developmental Editor: Cheryl Smith
Advertising/Promotions: Tom Fink
Production Editor: Lisa O'Conner
Cover Design: Alex Torres
Printed in the United States of America by KNI, Inc.

The Institute of Electrical and Electronics Engineers, Inc.

Preface

Making Multiple-Objective Decisions provides an overview of the most commonly used methods for solving decision problems that involve multiple attributes, goals, or objectives. The inspiration to write this book came from many sources, but perhaps the most important was a desire to give both graduate students and practitioners easy access to up-to-date information on multiple-criteria methods at an understandable level. This book was designed to accommodate newcomers to the field of multiple-criteria decision making by striving to make the concepts and theories easy to understand. Each method is briefly discussed, and simple and/or real-world examples are provided either in the text or in an annotated bibliography. The examples are provided to illustrate the usability of these methods in real decision problems.

The material in the book and the readings in the annotated bibliographies were originally selected as a supplement to a graduate-level Decision Analysis course offered in the Department of Industrial Engineering and Management Systems at the University of Central Florida. Every year, a number of managers and engineers who frequently need to make difficult multiple-criteria decisions have taken this course. The consensus is that the content of the book and the readings have provided them with useful insights into how to better structure decision problems, and how to analyze and justify the decisions made. Therefore, we feel that practicing managers, engineers, and computer scientists who are faced with complex and multiple-criteria decisions can benefit from this book. In addition, this book would provide an excellent supplement to Decision Analysis, Operations Research, and Operations Management courses offered in engineering and business schools.

The book is divided into five chapters. Chapter 1 provides an introduction to multicriteria decision making. This chapter includes a general discussion about the process of decision making, the types of multicriteria decision problems, and a classification of decision-making methods. The papers included in the annotated bibliography of Chapter 1 were selected to introduce the reader to the field of multicriteria decision making. In Chapter 2, we discuss a number of commonly used methods based on the prior articulation of preferences. After providing a discussion of each method, we include one or more application papers for each method in the annotated bibliography. Chapter 3 includes methods and application papers based on the progressive articulation of preferences. Chapter 4 includes an overview of the methods based on the posterior articulation of preferences. Data Envelopment Analysis (DEA) is also included in this chapter as one of the most widely used posterior methods. Finally, Chapter 5 provides the reader a guide to the selection and usage of the various methods. We conclude this chapter with an annotated bibliography containing a number of general papers on the usage as well as on the advantages and the disadvantages of the methods.

Special thanks go to our graduate students in the Decision Analysis and Advanced Engineering Economics courses over the past three years. This book owes its development to these graduate students because they were the main reasons for writing this book. They also provided valuable comments and suggestions during each offering of these courses. We greatly appreciate the help of our colleagues and friends, Dr. Gerald Evans and Dr. Robert Armacost, who provided valuable suggestions to enhance this work. We wish to express our gratitude to the anonymous reviewers of the original manuscript who provided invaluable comments and additions to the book. We also wish to express our appreciation to the IEEE Computer Society Press for their patience and assistance in making this book possible.

Table of Contents

Chapter 1   **Methods and Applications of Multicriteria Decision Making   1**

1.1   Introduction   1

1.2   The Process of Multiple-Criteria Decision Making (MCDM)   3

1.3   Multiple-Criteria Decision Problems   4

    1.3.1   Multiple-Objective Programming Problems   5
    1.3.2   Multiattribute Problems   6

1.4   Basic Terminology and Notation Used in MCDM   10

1.5   Classes of Solution Methodologies   11

    Annotated Bibliography   13

    References   14

Chapter 2   **Methods Based on the Prior Articulation of Preferences   17**

2.1   Introduction   17

2.2   Scoring Methods   17

2.3   Preference-Based Methods   21

    2.3.1   Multiattribute Value Functions   21
        2.3.1.1   The functional form of a value function   21
        2.3.1.2   Assessment of MAV functions   23
        2.3.1.3   Finding the best alternative   25
        2.3.1.4   Simple Multiattribute Rating Technique (SMART)   25
        2.3.1.5   A final note   26

    2.3.2   Multiattribute Utility Functions   26
        2.3.2.1   Axioms of utility theory   26
        2.3.2.2   Use of lotteries in assessing MAUT functions   27
        2.3.2.3   Functional forms of MAUT functions   28
        2.3.2.4   Assessment of MAUT functions   30
        2.3.2.5   Finding the best alternative   32

    2.3.3   Summary   33

2.4   The Analytic Hierarchy Process   33

2.5   Outranking Methods   41

    2.5.1   ELECTRE I   41
    2.5.2   ELECTRE II   46

2.6   Goal Programming   46

2.7   Summary   49

    Annotated Bibliography   50

    References   52

Chapter 3   **Methods Based on the Progressive Articulation of Preferences   55**

3.1   Introduction   55

    3.1.1   Methods Based on Weighting   55
    3.1.2   Constraint-Based Approaches   56
    3.1.3   Solution Methods   57

3.2   Interactive Surrogate Worth Trade-off Method   58

3.3   STEP Method   58

3.4   Geoffrion-Dyer-Feinberg (GDF) Method   60

3.5   Zionts and Wallenius Method   61

3.6   Tchebycheff Approach   62

3.7   Interactive and Visual Goal Programming   62

    Annotated Bibliography   63

    References   65

Chapter 4   **Methods Based on the Posterior Articulation of Preferences   67**

4.1   Introduction   37

4.2   Data Envelopment Analysis (DEA)   68

    4.2.1   The Basic Elements of DEA   68
    4.2.2   The DEA Linear Programming Formulation   70
    4.2.3   An Illustration of DEA   71

4.3   Concluding Remarks   74

    Annotated Bibliography   74

    References   75

Chapter 5   A Guide to Readers   77

5.1   Overview of Methods   77

5.2   Advantages and Disadvantages of MCDM methods   80

    5.2.1   Methods Based on the Prior Articulation of Preferences   80
    5.2.2   Methods Based on the Progressive Articulation of Preferences   82
    5.2.3   Methods Based on the Posterior Articulation of Preferences   85

5.3   A Guide for Selecting an MCDM Technique   86

Annotated Bibliography   90

References   91

Chapter 1

Methods and Applications of Multicriteria Decision Making

1.1 Introduction

Almost all decision problems involve the simultaneous consideration of several different objectives that are often in conflict. Consider, for example, a consumer who is considering the purchase of a new family car. The buyer may be concerned with the price of the car, its safety features, appearance, and engine efficiency. Clearly, an inexpensive safe car with great appearance and efficiency would be preferred by this person. However, these criteria are clearly in conflict since lower-priced cars usually do not include as many safety features as higher-priced cars do. Consequently, in order to determine the most preferred alternative, the buyer must be willing to make trade-offs among the various criteria. That is, the buyer must consider how much he is willing to pay in order to gain the additional safety features. In a manufacturing environment, a plant manager may be primarily interested in reducing the production costs; however, he or she may also be concerned with product diversification, short-term and long-term capital needs, and employee satisfaction (Goicoechea et al., 1982). These objectives are also clearly in conflict.

Multiple-criteria problems with conflicting objectives have been encountered in a number of different engineering applications. Quality control (Evans and Emberton, 1991), facility location (Cambron and Evans, 1991), project management (Bard, 1990; Mustafa and Al-Bahar, 1991; Hall et al., 1992), production control (Stam and Gardiner, 1992; Stam and Kuula, 1991), inventory planning (Kendall and Lee, 1980), and capital budgeting (Boucher and MacStravic, 1991) are just a few examples of problems

1

involving multiple criteria. Much effort has been devoted (and is still being devoted) to the development of methods to assist decision makers in such situations. In this book, we provide the reader with descriptions and examples of some of the more commonly used tools and techniques that can be used to aid decision makers in selecting the most preferred alternative in the presence of multiple conflicting objectives.

There is really nothing new about making decisions when multiple criteria are present—people have been making such decisions throughout history. Simple problems (such as those involving only a few objectives and a small number of alternatives) can usually be solved adequately without the use of sophisticated methods (that is, solved through the use of intuition or by various processes of choice). When the number of objectives and alternatives becomes large, however, the need for more formal (analytical) techniques becomes much more acute. In addition, formal techniques are often required for business and governmental decisions where there is a need to document and justify the decision process to large groups of people. In the presence of a large number of conflicting objectives and numerous alternatives, techniques that aid decision makers in structuring their preferences and values is very useful. These techniques are needed for such complex decision problems because it becomes very difficult for decision makers to articulate trade-off information and maintain some measure of consistency in their responses.

The development of multiple-criteria methods is actually relatively recent. Over the past 20 years there has been a plethora of tools and techniques developed for solving these problems. These methods are designed to clarify the decision problem, help generate useful alternative solutions, and help evaluate the alternatives based on a decision maker's values and preferences. They often involve the use of computer models.

The underlying theory of multiple-criteria decision making (MCDM) and algorithms has been summarized in a number of books, including Keeney and Raiffa (1976), Chankong and Haimes (1983), Zeleny (1982), Yu (1985), and Goicoechea et al. (1982). In general, these books describe the theoretical foundations for a large number of methods suitable for solving multiple criteria problems. Unfortunately, in most cases, a newcomer to the field of MCDM will find it very difficult to understand and apply these techniques in a practical problem setting. The majority of the decision problems and examples that are cited in such books and other operations-research literature (for example, the *Journal of the Operational Research Society*, *Management Science*, *Operations Research*, *Mathematics of OR*, *Decision Sciences*) involve small, simplified problems with only a few objectives. Therefore, one may encounter difficulties in trying to apply these methods to real-life applications. The purpose of this book is to provide the reader with sufficient background to understand and utilize some of the more commonly used methods in solving real-world decision problems. Throughout this book, we have tried to explain the methodologies in simple terms and provide examples to help the reader understand them better. Each chapter begins with brief overviews and examples of the techniques and then concludes with an annotated bibliography that includes real-world applications of these methods.

1.2 The Process of Multiple-Criteria Decision Making (MCDM)

Most decision situations include the following elements: (a) goals, objectives, and criteria to be achieved, (b) needs to be fulfilled, (c) constraints and requirements associated with and affected by the decision, (d) decision options or alternatives, (e) the environment in which the decision must be made, and (f) the experience and background of the decision maker(s). There are also a number of players involved in decision situations. The decision maker is the individual or group that has the authority to make the decision or approve the design. The stakeholders in a decision problem are the individuals or groups that can influence the decision and/or are affected by it. The analyst is a group or individual that synthesizes the subjective and objective inputs of the decision maker(s) and stakeholders into meaningful outputs that will aid in making a selection.

In general, a multiple-criteria problem begins when a decision maker has a situation that requires a decision. There may be a number of criteria that are of interest to the decision maker and the stakeholders involved in the problem. Several different courses of action may be available that address some or all of the criteria in some way. The problem facing the decision maker is to determine which course of action or alternative would best satisfy the criteria and fully satisfy the constraints.

The multicriteria decision-making process refers to the process of problem solving. Its purpose is to help the decision maker think systematically about complex decision problems and to improve the quality of the resulting decisions. It is important here to distinguish between a good decision and a good outcome from a decision. A good decision is one that is made based on a thorough understanding of the problem and careful analysis of the important aspects of the problem. Outcomes, on the other hand, may be lucky or unlucky. A decision resulting in a bad outcome could still be considered a good decision as long as the bad outcome was not totally unexpected by the decision maker. That is, the decision-making process must have indicated to the decision maker that there was a possibility of the poor outcome, and the decision maker must have weighed both the uncertainty and the pros and cons to reach an informed decision.

The decision-making process begins when the decision maker perceives a problem (for example, the need to alter the current system) or has a complex choice to make. The current situation is then diagnosed, and statements about the general needs or objectives are made. The process of defining the objectives may involve (a) describing the current state of the system, including both its good and bad features (sometimes called the descriptive scenario); (b) describing the preferred future state of the system (that is, what the system should look like once the problem is solved or a choice is made); (c) describing the needs and the wants (note that needs are necessary requirements while wants define desirable properties); (d) redefining the vague and disorganized list of wants (objectives) into a more operational and organized set of specific objectives (we describe an approach to this in Section 1.3.2); and (e) validating the list of objectives, making sure that all the essential elements of the problem have been included.

After defining the objectives, the next step in the process is to clearly identify the attributes (or performance measures) that relate to each objective. An attribute is a measurable quantity whose (measured) value reflects the degree of achievement for a particular objective. For example, an objective may be to minimize cost, and the associated attribute could be measured in dollars. The values of an attribute associated with an objective may be given by a model, measured directly, or assessed subjectively. For example, when choosing from among a number of different products at different production levels, the dollar cost associated with each product mix can be computed using an explicit function of the numbers of each of the product types. Other attributes are directly measurable, observable, or subjectively assessed (such as color, gas mileage, and comfort of a set of alternative cars).

Once the attributes or performance measures have been defined, a set of candidate alternatives for achieving the objectives is determined. These alternatives may be implicitly described in terms of variables (for example, alternative box designs can be defined implicitly in terms of their lengths, widths, and heights) or they may be given explicitly (for example, alternative cars include the Ford Mustang, Honda Accord, and so on).

After the set of alternatives has been defined and the attributes have been determined, then the analysis and evaluation step begins. Each alternative is evaluated relative to others in terms of a prespecified set of decision rules. The alternative with the highest rank according to the decision rule is chosen for implementation. Plans for implementation are then made. In some situations, after performing the analysis and evaluation step, it may be found that none of the alternatives is satisfactory. This could occur, for example, if the constraints are too restrictive or if an insufficient set of alternatives has been generated. This can also occur if the current decision model is not requisite. A requisite decision model is one that contains everything that is essential for solving the problem. When no satisfactory alternative can be found, then one would return to the problem/goal definition stage and repeat the process.

There are a large number of methods available for the analysis and evaluation step of the decision-making process. The application of these methods, however, depends on the type of problem, which is the focus of the following section.

1.3 Multiple-Criteria Decision Problems

Problems involving multiple criteria are broadly classified into two types: (1) multiple-objective programming problems refer to problems that have a very large number of feasible alternatives, as described through the use of decision variables, where the objectives and the constraints are functionally related to the decision variables, and (2) multiple-attribute problems refer to problems that have a relatively small number of alternatives, where the alternatives are represented in terms of attributes.

Multiobjective mathematical programming is one way of considering multiple objectives explicitly and simultaneously in a mathematical programming framework. Its foundations began with the work of Pareto (1896). The development of necessary and sufficient conditions for a solution to be optimal to a vector maximization problem occurred in the early 1950s (Kuhn and Tucker, 1951).

The multiple-attribute methods began with the work of Churchman and Ackoff (1954) and were axiomatized by Debreu (1960), Luce and Tukey (1964), Krantz (1964), and Scott (1964). Following this earlier work, the developments in the 1970s, '80s, and '90s have been in both multiple-objective programming and multiattribute decision making.

1.3.1 Multiple-Objective Programming Problems

Multiple-objective programming problems generally involve maximizing $p > 1$ objective functions defined over a set of feasible decisions. Mathematically, this problem is defined as:

$$\text{Maximize} \quad f(x) = \left[f_1(x), f_2(x), \ldots, f_p(x) \right]$$
$$\text{subject to} \quad g_j(x) \leq 0 \qquad j = 1, 2, \ldots, m \tag{1-1}$$

where

x is an n-dimensional vector of decision variables,

$f_i(x), i = 1, 2, \ldots, p$ are p distinct objective functions, and

$g_j(x), j = 1, 2, \ldots, m$ are m distinct constraint functions.

Although the problem given in Equation (1-1) appears to be very restrictive in that it requires the maximization of each of the objectives and all of its constraints are of the "less-than" type, it is actually quite general. For example, if an objective function is used where lower values are preferred (for example, minimize cost), then the negative of this function can be used in Equation (1-1) to be maximized. In a similar fashion, a greater-than constraint can be transformed into a less than constraint by taking its negative. If a constraint needs to be satisfied exactly (an equality constraint), it can be represented through the use of two inequalities.

Because of the conflicting nature of the objectives given in Equation (1-1), a single setting of the decision variables, x, will not maximize all of the objectives simultaneously. Instead, we will find that some solutions are good in some of the objectives and not in others, whereas other solutions are better for a different subset of the objectives. If solutions are found that are worse in at least one objective and the same in the remaining objectives when compared to another feasible solution, then this set of "dominated" solutions can be eliminated. In general, this elimination process will lead to a set of nondominated solutions where there is no clear winner in all of the objectives. The (nondominated) solution selected by the decision maker is referred to as a "best-compromise solution" or "satisfactory solution," rather than a "superior solution" or "optimal solution." It is obvious that two distinct decision makers with their unique sets of values will likely choose different best-compromise solutions.

In choosing a solution, the decision maker must be willing to accept a loss in one or more of the objectives in order to increase another objective—this is commonly referred to as making trade-offs among the objectives. This trade-off information is often very difficult to elicit, especially when there is a large number of criteria. With the use of more formalized techniques, however, the decision maker is guided throughout the process in order to reduce the cognitive burden and to improve consistency.

As an example of a multiobjective problem, consider a manufacturer who would like to produce three independent products but is not sure how many of each to produce. Each product requires a set amount of the available resources (such as machine time, labor time, raw material), while each contributes differently to the overall profit of the company. In addition, there is a projected demand for each of the products and some of the resources are considered to be more scarce than others. Since the manager would like to determine how many of each of the products to produce, the decision variables in this product mix problem are the number of units of products 1, 2, and 3 to be produced. The objectives of this problem could include maximizing profit, minimizing the deviation from contract demand requirements for each product, and minimizing scarce resource consumption. Unfortunately, some of these objectives could be conflicting in nature and it is impossible to find a solution that optimizes all objectives simultaneously when they conflict. For example, maximizing profit would require higher resource usage, whereas minimizing scarce resource consumption obviously requires lower resource usage. In such cases, one may seek what is referred to as a "satisfactory solution" or "best-compromise solution." One way to achieve a satisfactory solution is to use goal programming (GP). GP allows the decision maker to specify a target for each objective function. For example, $100,000 is a target for profit. The method then finds a solution by minimizing the sum of the deviations of each objective from its target value. Of course, the decision maker can also assign priorities and weights to each objective. The different values of priorities and weights, which represent the decision maker's preferences, will lead to distinct preferred solutions. Goal programming is described in detail in Chapter 2.

Note that the objectives of the product mix problem stated above can all be expressed mathematically in terms of the decision variables (that is, they are functions of the number of items of each type produced). This is a necessary requirement for a problem to be stated as a multiobjective problem. Not all decision problems can take this form. The following section describes the other main class of multiple-criteria problems.

1.3.2 Multiattribute Problems

Multiattribute decision problems generally involve a finite set of n alternatives and a relatively large set of p attributes. The goal here can be (a) to help the decision maker choose the best action or alternative of those studied (a choice or selection procedure), (b) to help sort out alternatives that seem "good" among a set of alternatives studied (a sorting or segmentation procedure), and/or (c) to help rank the alternatives in decreasing order of preference (an ordering or ranking procedure) (Colson and De Bruyn, 1989).

In order to solve multiattribute problems, one must first select the appropriate attributes that will provide the basis for evaluating the set of alternatives. The decision maker must then determine the importance of the criteria (attributes) and assign corresponding weights to them, and then rank the alternatives with respect to the criteria. The determination of these measures leads to an ordinal or cardinal ranking of the alternatives.

The selection and structuring of attributes is one of the most difficult as well as one of the most critical steps in solving multiattribute problems. In selecting attributes one must identify those factors that are important for the particular decision problem at hand. Some attributes may be fairly easy to measure directly, such as the cost and gas mileage of a car. Other attributes, such as the comfort level of a car, may be more difficult to measure directly. The level of comfort may be assessed subjectively on a rating scale or by use of a set of proxy attributes (for example, stiffness of the suspension, noise level in decibels, and so on).

There is no ideal number of attributes that should be considered. Specifying too few attributes may mean that some important ones have not been included, while specifying too many attributes may mean that too much detail has been included in the problem. In the latter case, one can reduce the number of attributes to a manageable number by omitting those that have no significant effect in the final selection of an alternative (Canada and Sullivan, 1989).

There are a number of important characteristics of a good attribute or set of attributes (see Keeney and Raiffa, 1976). An attribute should be comprehensive (that is, its value should be indicative of the degree to which the objective is met) and measurable (it should be relatively easy to assign it a scaled value). The set of attributes should be complete (that is, all pertinent aspects of the decision problem should be represented), operational (you should be able to use the attributes in some meaningful way in the subsequent analyses), decomposable (they should simplify the decision process by disaggregating the problem into easier-to-handle parts), nonredundant (no part of the decision problem should be accounted for more than once), and minimal (no other, smaller set of attributes should describe the same decision problem). A particular multiattribute method may also have additional attribute requirements. For example, one of the important requirements for using an additive function in multiattribute utility theory is that the attributes must be mutually preferentially independent of one another. We will discuss this in more detail in Chapter 2.

Once the attributes have been selected, it may be helpful to structure them into a hierarchy; this is particularly useful when the number of attributes is large. Because simultaneous assessment of a large number of attributes can be a very difficult task, grouping the common attributes may facilitate the process. One approach that can be used in the structuring of attributes is the development of an objectives tree (Gibson, 1992). The objectives tree is a graphical display of the goals (or attributes) of the system.

The first step in developing the objectives tree is to state the overall project goal along with the primary factors (attributes) that influence the achievement of that goal.

The development of the objectives tree is simplified by identifying and stating the goals in a specific semantic format. In particular, the following semantic structure is used:

To (Action Word) + (Object) + (Qualifying Words)

For example, the quality of a car may be an important attribute when deciding what car to purchase. In order to state the attribute "quality" as a goal in its proper semantic format, we attach an action word and qualifying words as follows:

To (maximize) (the quality) (of the selected car)

After listing the factors in the proper semantic form, they are arranged in a hierarchy where higher or more general goals are listed above the more specific goals. Note that a subgoal "will assist in" or "will help to achieve" a higher-level goal and that a higher-level goal "includes" or "implies" the subgoals. Figure 1.1 shows an example of an objectives tree used to aid in the selection of graphical techniques for work-methods improvement (Stanney et al., 1994).

After the hierarchy is developed, the following four tests recommended by Gibson (1992) can be used to check the logic of the objectives tree:

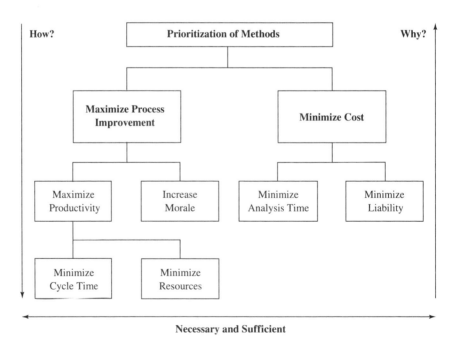

Figure 1.1   An Example of an Objectives Tree

1. Reading "down" any branch, each goal must answer the "**how**" of its immediately higher goal. For example, **how** do we maximize process improvement? Process improvement is maximized by maximizing productivity and by increasing morale.

2. Reading "up" any branch, each higher goal answers "**why**" the goal above it is needed. For example, **why** is it important to minimize analysis time? We want to minimize the analysis time in order to minimize costs.

3. Reading "across" the goals at a given level under any one general goal, the question, Are all the more specific goals **necessary** to accomplish the more general goal? must be asked. For example, are both minimizing cycle time and minimizing resources **necessary** to maximize productivity?

4. Reading "across" the goals at a given level under any one general goal, the question, Are the specific goals at this level **sufficient** to accomplish the more general goal? must be asked. For example, are considerations of cost and process improvement **sufficient** to prioritize methods-improvement techniques?

The above tests ensure the logical flow of the hierarchy. If any of the above four tests fails, then suitable modifications to the hierarchy are made and the process is repeated. The success of the approach, however, depends on working closely with the decision maker to ensure that the goals and their respective criticalities are accurately reflected in the hierarchy. The greater the involvement of the decision maker in the process, the more likely it is for the decision model to be requisite.

As a simple example of a multiattribute problem, consider the decision of selecting a car from among four domestic automobiles based on attributes such as cost, performance, gas mileage, and appearance. The four automobiles, shown in Table 1.1, are the alternatives under consideration. Each alternative is characterized by the set of attributes, and unlike the multiobjective problems, these alternatives cannot be described mathematically in terms of decision variables. Note that although a hierarchy is not presented here, it may be useful to develop a hierarchy so that both appearance and performance can be further clarified. For example, we might ask the question: "How is

Table 1.1 An Example of a Simple Multiattribute Problem

Criteria	Alternatives			
	Car 1	Car 2	Car 3	Car 4
Price	30K	25K	20K	15K
MPG	Low	Medium	Medium	High
Appearance	Great	Acceptable	Great	Acceptable
Performance	High	High	Moderate	Moderate

performance maximized?" One may respond, for example, "Performance is maximized by maximizing acceleration and horsepower."

It should be obvious that the above criteria cannot all be optimized simultaneously; that is, none of the four alternative cars has the best values for each criterion. The objective here is to select the car that maximizes the decision maker's preferences based on the stated criteria. A number of approaches, such as the analytic hierarchy process (AHP) (Saaty, 1994), outranking methods (Benayoun et al., 1966; Roy, 1975), and scoring methods (Moore and Baker, 1969; Suresh and Meredith, 1985) can be used to solve this problem. Multiple-objective mathematical programming techniques such as goal programming and multiobjective programming are not appropriate for solving this problem because a functional relationship does not exist among the criteria and the alternatives. In general, multiattribute methods (such as AHP, scoring methods, and outranking) are not interchangeable with multiobjective programming methods (MOP). However, they can sometimes be used in a complementary fashion where MOP is used to find a finite number of nondominated solutions and then a multiattribute method is used to select the most preferred one. These techniques will be described in detail in Chapters 2 and 3.

1.4 Basic Terminology and Notation Used in MCDM

Before describing the classes of solution methodologies, we provide some general concepts and definitions that are commonly cited in the literature in discussions of MCDM problems and approaches.

- *Pareto Optimal (Nondominated or Efficient) Solution:* Let X be the set of all feasible solutions. An efficient (nondominated) solution is a feasible solution, $x^* \in X$, for which there does not exist any other feasible solution, $x \in X$, that is the same or better in each of the objectives. In other words, you can not find another solution x where $f_i(x) \geq f_i(x^*)$ for $i = 1, 2, \ldots, p$ and for at least one i, $f_i(x) > f_i(x^*)$. (Note that we are assuming that higher values of $f_i(x)$ are preferred.) Clearly, an efficient solution is, in general, not unique. The collection of all efficient solutions is a subset of the feasible region in the decision space.

- *Superior Solution:* A superior solution is one that maximizes all of the objectives simultaneously; a solution x^0 is superior if and only if for $x^0 \in X$, $f_i(x^0) \geq f_i(x)$ for all i, and all $x \in X$.

  Because of the conflicting nature of most objectives (that is, improvement in one objective results in the deterioration of another), a superior solution seldom exists. Therefore, the decision maker is faced with the problem of deciding how much of one objective to give up in order to gain in another. This becomes a problem involving value trade-offs among the objectives. Later in this book, we will demonstrate how to use trade-offs to solve problems of conflicting objectives.

- *Most Preferred (Best-Compromise) Solution:* A best-compromise solution is an efficient solution chosen as the final solution based on the decision maker's overall preference function. Note that the best-compromise solution to a problem chosen by one decision maker will most likely be different from the best-compromise solution to the same problem chosen by another decision maker.

- *Trade-off or Marginal Rate of Substitution:* The trade-off ratio, or marginal rate of substitution, between objectives f_1 and f_2 at a given point is the ratio $(\partial U/\partial f_1)/(\partial U/\partial f_2)$. Here, the function U represents the utility (preference structure) of the decision maker defined in terms of the functions f_1 and f_2. The meaning of this ratio is that when $(\partial U/\partial f_1)/(\partial U/\partial f_2) = r$ at a given point, the decision maker is indifferent to a decrement of r units in f_1 as long as f_2 is incremented by one unit. This ratio generally depends on the levels of f_1 and f_2 and sometimes on the levels of the other objectives. This concept is described in the algorithms presented in Chapter 3.

- *Ordinal Ranking versus Cardinal Ranking:* Ordinal ranking provides only an order ranking of the alternatives. For instance, when comparing two alternatives, an ordinal ranking would only lead to a determination that alternative A is preferred to alternative B, but not by how much. Cardinal ranking, on the other hand, specifies not only that alternative A is preferred to B, but also by how much.

- *Aspiration Levels, Goals:* An aspiration level is a specific value that defines a desirable level of an objective. A goal is the result of using an objective in conjunction with an aspiration value. For instance, if a decision maker specifies that he desires to achieve a profit of $1,000, then the value of 1,000 is his aspiration level and his desire to achieve that level of profit is a clearly stated goal.

1.5 Classes of Solution Methodologies

Based on the classification given in Evans (1984), almost all methods for solving multiple-criteria problems (whether multiple-objective or multiattribute) involve two general subprocesses: (1) articulation of the decision maker's preference structure over the multiple criteria, and (2) optimization of the preference structure. Thus, the various methods can be categorized according to the timing of these subprocesses relative to one another: (1) prior articulation of preferences (in which the preference structure is obtained prior to the optimization), (2) progressive articulation of preferences (in which the elicitation of information about the preference structure is interspersed with the optimization), and (3) posterior articulation of preferences (in which the decision maker's preference is elicited after the generation of the nondominated solutions).

Techniques based on the *prior articulation of preferences* include, for example, goal programming and the use of a multiattribute value function or a multiattribute utility function. Basically, in these approaches the decision maker's preferences are obtained through detailed interviews between the decision maker and the analyst prior to the start of the optimization process. The major disadvantage of this approach is the difficulty facing the decision maker in giving the required preference information. The optimization process, however, is usually relatively simple because the multiple-criteria problem has typically been reduced to a single-objective problem.

Techniques characterized by the *progressive articulation of preferences* (interactive methods) often involve an interaction between the decision maker and the computer (and analyst) throughout the process. These methods follow a general pattern. The decision maker provides some local information regarding his or her preferences over the multidimensional outcome space. This information allows the formulation of a single criterion subproblem, which is then solved. The new solution and the outcome (values of the criteria) are then presented to the decision maker, who provides new local information about his or her preferences. This process is repeated until the decision maker either converges toward a best-compromise solution or terminates the process prior to reaching this point. The objective of this approach is to find a satisfactory solution after a reasonable number of iterations and within a reasonable amount of time.

When compared to the prior articulation of preferences methods, interactive procedures are, in general, more complicated and difficult for the decision maker to understand. These methods tend to involve a higher degree of mathematical sophistication and, consequently, are less transparent to the user. However, they require less information from the decision maker in terms of implementation. An advantage of these methods is that they are interactive in nature and require the information to be obtained incrementally. This means that the decision maker is involved throughout the process. Of course, there are various degrees of difficulty associated with the different types of information required from the decision maker. This information could range from providing a simple ranking to a more difficult assessment of marginal rates of substitution. The preferred methods are obviously those that avoid placing excessive demands on the decision maker.

Algorithms that rely on the *posterior articulation of preferences* seek first to find all or almost all of the nondominated solutions to the problem. These solutions are then presented to the decision maker to select the preferred one through some further process. There are several disadvantages to this class of methods. First, the algorithms are often very complex and difficult for the analyst and the decision maker to understand and use. Second, many real-world problems, particularly multiple-objective programming problems, are too large to be solved using this approach. Finally, posterior methods can lead to a very large number of efficient (nondominated) solutions. Choosing a single preferred solution from a large efficient set can be a very difficult task for the decision maker. There are, however, techniques available for reducing a large set of nondominated solutions to a manageable number (see, for example, Graves et al., 1992).

Among the three classes of methods, techniques within the prior articulation class (such as scoring methods and the analytic hierarchy process) seem to be the most widely used. This is especially true of the methods in practice in the United States. In Europe, however, some of the interactive methods (for example, Visual Interactive

Goal Programming; Korhonen, 1987) appear to be more widely used. In general, because of the difficulties discussed earlier, the posterior methods are the least widely used. Data envelopment analysis (DEA) is a relatively new approach to analyzing the relative efficiency of a set of alternatives in a multiattribute problem. This approach has received wide attention as evidenced by its recent inclusion in a mathematical programming book by Winston (1995) and the proliferation of application papers in the literature (Seiford, 1990). Because DEA is used to analyze the entire set of nondominated solutions, we have elected to classify it as a posterior method.

The organization of this book is as follows. Chapter 2 provides an overview and examples of the more commonly used methods based on the prior articulation of preferences. Chapter 3 discusses several methods based on the progressive articulation of preferences. In Chapter 4, a brief overview of DEA is given. Finally, in Chapter 5, we provide a guide for selecting an appropriate MCDM method given a decision problem. Each chapter is concluded with an annotated bibliography of related readings. These readings have been selected to illustrate the application of MCDM methods in real-world settings and to provide some general-interest papers as an introduction to MCDM and its usage.

Annotated Bibliography

Buede, D.M., "Structuring Value Attributes," *Interfaces*, Vol. 16, No. 2, 1986, pp. 52–62.

Summary: This paper discusses the art of structuring decision problems. The author emphasizes the importance of identifying the value attributes in the analysis of such problems. He discusses two systematic methods for structuring decision problems—a top-down objective-driven approach and a bottom-up alternative-driven approach.

Dyer, J.S., Fishburn, P.C., Steuer, R.E., Wallenius, J., and S. Zionts, "Multiple Criteria Decision Making, Multiattribute Utility Theory: The Next Ten Years," *Management Science*, Vol. 38, No. 5, 1992, pp. 645–653.

Summary: This paper focuses on the future of multiple-criteria decision making. It discusses the past contributions made, followed by a discussion of promising topics and new research areas. The authors describe new research directions in terms of decision support systems, behavioral realities, decision heuristics, and the use of computer software for solving such decision problems.

Evans, G.W., "An Overview of Techniques for Solving Multiobjective Mathematical Programs," *Management Science*, Vol. 30, No. 11, 1984, pp. 1268–1282.

Summary: This paper provides an overview of techniques for solving multiple-objective programming problems. The author classifies the techniques based on the timing of the articulation of preferences versus the optimization process and discusses the advantages and disadvantages of each approach. In addition, he provides a comprehensive review of methods developed in each class of techniques.

Keeney, R.L., "Using Values in Operations Research," *Operations Research*, Vol. 42, No. 5, 1994, pp. 793–813.

Summary: This paper discusses the importance of values (that is, the quantification of attributes, objectives, and/or criteria) in multicriteria decision problems. More specifically, it provides the reader with an understanding of how values guide the entire decision process. The author provides valuable insight into how to identify the attributes and objectives, how to structure these attributes to facilitate the analysis, how to create better alternatives, how to quantify the values, and then how these values guide and integrate the entire decision process.

Keller, L.R., and J.L. Ho, "Decision Problem Structuring: Generating Options," *IEEE Trans. Systems, Man, and Cybernetics*, IEEE CS Press, Los Alamitos, Calif., Vol. 18, No. 5, 1988, pp. 715–727.

Summary: This paper provides an integrative framework for generating alternatives in multicriteria decision problems. Five categories of option-generating procedures are discussed. In addition, an approach is described that determines whether additional options need to be included in the decision problem.

Rosenthal, R.E., "Concepts, Theory, and Techniques—Principles of Multiobjective Optimization," *Decision Sciences*, Vol. 16, 1985, pp. 133–152.

Summary: This paper provides a discussion of the underlying theoretical principles of multiple-objective decision making. The author provides the reader with the basic terminology and definitions used and discusses several of the multiple-objective optimization techniques.

References

Bard, J.F., "Using Multicriteria Methods in the Early Stages of New Product Development," *J. Operational Research Soc.*, Vol. 41, No. 8, 1990, pp. 755–766.

Benayoun, R., Roy, B., and B. Sussman, "ELECTRE: Une Méthode Pour Guider le Choix en Présence de Points de Vue Multiples," *sema* (Metra International), Direction Scientifique, Note de Travail No. 49, June 1966.

Boucher, T.O., and E.L. MacStravic, "Multiattribute Evaluation Within a Present Value Framework and Its Relation to the Analytic Hierarchy Process," *The Eng. Economist*, Vol. 37, No. 1, 1991, pp. 1–32.

Canada, J.R., and W.G. Sullivan, *Economic and Multiattribute Evaluation of Advanced Manufacturing Systems*, Prentice Hall, Englewood Cliffs, N.J., 1989.

Cambron, K., and G.W. Evans, "Use of the Analytic Hierarchy Process for Multiobjective Facility Layout," *Computers and Industrial Eng.*, Vol. 20, 1991, pp. 211–229.

Chankong, V., and Y.Y. Haimes, *Multiobjective Decision Making: Theory and Methodology, Elsevier*, North-Holland Publishing, New York, 1983.

Churchman, C.W. and R.L. Ackoff, "An Approximate Measure of Value," *Operations Research*, Vol. 2, 1954, pp. 172–187.

Colson, G., and C. De Bruyn, "Models and Methods in Multiple Objectives Decision Making," *Math. Computer Modeling*, Vol. 12, No. 10/11, 1989, pp. 1201–1211.

Debreu, G., "Topological Methods in Cardinal Utility Theory," In K.J. Arrow, S. Karlin and P. Suppes (eds.), *Mathematical Methods in the Social Sciences 1959*, Stanford Univ. Press, Stanford, Calif., 1960, pp. 16–26.

Evans, G.W., "An Overview of Techniques for Solving Multiobjective Mathematical Programs," *Management Science*, Vol. 30, No. 11, 1984, pp. 1268–1282.

Evans, G.W., and G.R. Emberton, "Bicriterion Design of Process Control Charts," *Int'l J. Production Economics*, Vol. 22, 1991, pp. 141–150.

Gibson, J., *How to Do Systems Analysis*, unpublished manuscript, Prentice Hall, Englewood Cliffs, N.J., 1992.

Goicoechea, A., Hansen, D. R., and L. Duckstein, *Multiobjective Decision Analysis with Engineering and Business Applications*, John Wiley & Sons, New York, 1982.

Graves, S.B., Ringuest, J.L., and J. Bard, "Recent Developments in Screening Methods for Nondominated Solutions in Multiobjective Optimization," *Computers and Operations Research*, Vol. 19, No. 7, 1992, pp. 683–694.

Hall, N.G., Hershey, J.C., Kessler, L.G., and R.C. Stotts, "A Model for Making Project Funding Decisions at the National Cancer Institute," *Operations Research*, Vol. 40, No. 6, 1992, pp. 1040–1052.

Keeney, R.L., and H. Raiffa, *Decisions with Multiple Objectives: Preferences and Value Trade-offs*, Wiley, New York, 1976.

Kendall, K.E., and S.M. Lee, "Formulating Blood Rotation Policies with Multiple Objectives," *Management Science*, Vol. 26, No. 11, 1980, pp. 1145–1157.

Korhonen, P., "VIG—A Visual Interactive Support System for Multiple Criteria Decision Making," *Belgian J. Operations Research, Statistics, and Computer Science*, Vol. 27, 1987, pp. 3–15.

Krantz, D.H., "Conjoint Measurement: The Luce-Tukey Axiomatization and Some Extensions," *J. Math. Psychology*, Vol. 1, 1964, pp. 248–277.

Kuhn, H.W. and A.W. Tucker, "Nonlinear Programming," *Proc. 2nd Berkeley Symp. Math. Statistics and Probability*, Berkeley, Calif., 1951, pp. 481–492.

Luce, R.D. and J.W. Tukey, "Simultaneous Conjoint Measurement: A New Type of Fundamental Measurement," *J. Math. Psychology*, 1964, pp. 1–27.

Moore, J.R., and N.R. Baker, "Scoring Models for R&D Project Selection," *Management Science*, Vol. 16, No. 4, 1969, pp. B212–B232.

Mustafa, M., and J. Al-Bahar, "Project Risk Assessment Using the Analytic Hierarchy Process," *IEEE Trans. Eng. Management*, IEEE CS Press, Los Alamitos, Calif., Vol. 38, No. 1, 1991, pp. 46–52.

Pareto, V., *Cours d'Economie Politique*, Rouge, Lausanne, Switzerland, 1896.

Roy, B., "Why Multicriteria Decision Aid May Not Fit in with the Assessment of a Unique Criteria," in M. Zeleny (ed.), *Multiple Criteria Decision Making*, Springer-Verlag, New York, 1975, pp. 280–283.

Saaty, T.L., "How to Make a Decision: The Analytic Hierarchy Process," *Interfaces*, Vol. 24, No. 6, 1994, pp. 19–43.

Scott, D., "Measurement Structures and Linear Inequalities," *J. Math. Psychology*, Vol. 1, 1964, pp. 233–247.

Seiford, L.M., "A Bibliography of Data Envelopment Analysis (1978–1990), Version 5, Tech. report, Dept. Industrial Eng. and Operations Research, Univ. of Massachusetts, Amherst, Mass., 1990.

Stam, A., and L. Gardiner, "A Multiple Objective Marketing-Manufacturing Approach for Order (Market) Selection," *Computers and Operation Research*, Vol. 19, No. 7, 1992, pp. 571–583.

Stam, A., and M. Kuula, "Selecting a Flexible Manufacturing System Using Multiple Criteria Analysis," *Int'l J. Production Research*, Vol. 29, No. 4, 1991, pp. 803–820.

Stanney, K.M., Pet-Edwards, J., Swart, W. W., Safford, R., and T. Barth, "The Design of a Systematic Methods Improvement Planning Methodology: Part II—A Multiattribute Utility Theory (MAUT) Approach," *Int'l J. Industrial Engineering*, Vol. 1, No. 4, 1994, pp. 275–284.

Suresh, N.C., and J.R. Meredith, "Justifying Multimachine Systems: An Integrated Strategic Approach," *J. Manufacturing Systems*, Vol. 4, No. 2, 1985, pp. 212–229.

Winston, W.L., *Introduction to Mathematical Programming*, Duxbury Press, Belmont, Calif., 1995.

Yu, P.L., *Multiple Criteria Decision Making: Concepts, Techniques, and Extensions*, Plenum, New York, 1985.

Zeleny, M., *Multiple Criteria Decision Making*, McGraw-Hill, New York, 1982.

Chapter 2

Methods Based on the Prior Articulation of Preferences

2.1 Introduction

In this chapter, we describe a variety of MCDM approaches that are based on the prior articulation of preferences, where the preference structure is obtained prior to the start of the optimization process. Some of these approaches are suitable for solving only multiattribute problems (for example, scoring methods, the analytic hierarchy process, and outranking methods), some are suitable only for multiple-objective programming problems (such as goal programming), while others can be used for both multiattribute and multiple objective programming problems (for example, utility-based methods). The majority of the approaches are designed for problems with known (deterministic) outcomes. Table 2.1 summarizes the methods described in the chapter.

2.2 Scoring Methods

Scoring methods are one of the simplest and probably one of the most popular tools for solving multiattribute decision problems. These methods first assign weights to the criteria and then rate the alternatives against each criterion. In general, there are two types of "weighting and rating" methods. The first is an empirical approach where the weights are arbitrarily assigned or derived from some ad hoc procedure. The second is an axiomatic approach where weights are derived from procedures that have theoretical foundations (for example, analytic hierarchy process). There are a number of

Table 2.1 Summary of Methods Based on Prior Articulation of Preferences

Methods based on prior articulation of preferences	Type of problem	Type of output
Scoring Methods	Multiattribute, Deterministic	Ordinal Ranking
Multiattribute Value Functions	Multiattribute and Multiple-Objective, Deterministic	Cardinal Ranking
Multiattribute Utility Functions	Multiattribute and Multiple-Objective, Uncertain Outcomes	Cardinal Ranking
Analytic Hierarchy Process	Multiattribute, Deterministic	Cardinal Ranking (ratio scale)
Outranking Methods	Multiattribute, Deterministic	Partial or Complete Ordinal Ranking
Goal Programming	Multiple-Objective, Deterministic	Identifies "best-compromise solution"

different types of methods within each of these two categories. In this section, we describe and illustrate a simple empirical scoring method used by Kepner and Tregoe (1981) in their problem solving seminars.

Recall that a multiattribute problem consists of a list of n alternatives from which the decision maker chooses the most preferred option based on the m attributes of the alternatives. In the scoring method used by Kepner and Tregoe, the decision maker first assigns weights, w_i $(i = 1, \ldots, m)$, to each of the m attributes. In order to assess these weights, the relative importance of each attribute is determined on a scale of 1 to 10 or 1 to 100. The decision maker should first decide on the range of the scale to use. A wider range (such as, 1 to 100) will allow the decision maker to give greater differentiation among the attributes. Note that these scales do not include a value of zero. This is because the value of zero for a weight on an attribute would imply that the attribute has zero importance to the decision problem. If this were the case, then the attribute should not have been included in the first place.

After selecting a scale, the decision maker determines which of the attributes is most important and assigns the highest value to that attribute (thus, 10 or 100, depending on the scale). The importance of the remaining attributes is then assessed relative to the one with the highest weight by assigning a weight between 1 and the upper limit of the scale to each.

In the next step, the decision maker evaluates how well each of the n alternatives performs with respect to each of the m attributes. In order to accomplish this, a numerical value, a_{ij} $(i = 1, \ldots, m; j = 1, \ldots, n)$, is assigned to indicate the degree to which each alternative achieves each attribute. Again, the decision maker must first select a scale to use (usually either 0 to 10 or 0 to 100). When evaluating how well an alternative performs with respect to an attribute, the value of zero can be included because a particular alternative may not include a certain feature (attribute). Once the scale is selected, the decision maker determines the alternative that achieves the best value for the first attribute and assigns the highest score to that alternative. Then the remaining alternatives are evaluated relative to the alternative with the highest attribute score. This process is repeated for all m attributes.

The worth, v_j, of the jth alternative is obtained by the following weighted sum:

$$v_j = \sum_{i=1}^{m} w_i a_{ij} \qquad j = 1, 2, \ldots, n \qquad (2\text{-}1)$$

The alternative j with the highest value of v_j is selected as the best option.

The following example demonstrates this scoring method. Consider a car buyer who is making a selection from among four cars. The attributes under consideration are the price of each car, gas mileage in miles per gallon (MPG), appearance, and performance. Table 2.2 summarizes the pertinent information about each alternative. The first step is for the buyer to score the attributes. Suppose that the buyer selects the 1-to-10 scale for scoring the attributes and that the price is considered to be the most important attribute. Further suppose that the cars' gas mileage is a close second, performance is about half as important as price, and appearance is slightly less important than performance. The following responses by the buyer for the attribute weights would be consistent with the preceding preferences: 10, 8, 4, 5, respectively.

The next step is for the buyer to associate a degree of importance representing how well each alternative achieves each of the attributes. Suppose that the buyer chooses to assign numerical scores between 0 and 10. The buyer now considers each attribute and determines which alternative receives the highest score, scoring the remaining alternatives with respect to the one receiving the highest score. For example, a score of 10 is

Table 2.2   An Example of a Scoring Problem

Criteria	Alternatives			
	Car 1	Car 2	Car 3	Car 4
Price	30K	25K	20K	15K
MPG	Low	Medium	Medium	High
Appearance	Great	Acceptable	Great	Acceptable
Performance	High	High	Moderate	Moderate

Table 2.3 Alternative Scores with Respect
to Each Attribute

Criteria	Alternatives			
	Car 1	Car 2	Car 3	Car 4
Price	3	5	7	10
MPG	5	8	8	10
Appearance	10	5	10	5
Performance	10	10	4	4

assigned to the price of car 4 because car 4 has the lowest price among all the cars (that is, it would be most preferred in terms of price). The buyer then assigns a score of 3 to the price of car 1 to reflect that the price of car 4 is approximately 3 times more attractive than the price of car 1. This process is repeated for each of the cars and each of the attributes. Table 2.3 contains the buyer's assessed scores for each alternative with respect to each attribute. Equation (2-1) is then used to derive the value of each alternative. The value of alternative 1, for example, is calculated as

$$\nu_1 = (10 \cdot 3) + (8 \cdot 5) + (4 \cdot 10) + (5 \cdot 10)$$

$$\nu_1 = 160$$

In this example, car 4 results in the highest value (220) and is the best choice for this particular car buyer. Cars 2 and 3 have fairly close scores of 184 and 194, respectively. Note that with a slight modification of the weights (for example, if performance is given a weight of 7 instead of 5) the preference order between cars 2 and 3 will be reversed. It is important that the decision maker be made aware of the sensitivity of the outcomes (that is, how easily the ordering of the alternatives changes) to small changes in the assessed scores and weights.

Scoring methods tend to be rather ad hoc because the interpretation of the scales is not prespecified and the scales are often misinterpreted as a ranking rather than as a relative importance. In addition, the scores on the attributes are not truly weights. Consequently, the use of the linear weighted sum to compute the values of the alternatives has little theoretical foundation to support it. However, because they are easy to use, scoring methods are actually quite widely applied in real-world settings. For example, Kepner and Tregoe have been advocating the use of these methods for over 35 years. In addition, scoring methods have the benefit of helping the decision maker structure and analyze the decision problem.

The remaining methods described in this chapter have stronger theoretical foundations but are more difficult to use. These methods include preference-based techniques, the analytic hierarchy process, outranking methods, and goal programming.

2.3 Preference-Based Methods

Preference-based methods are used to solve multiattribute and multiple-objective decision problems where it is desirable to rank a set of alternatives. These methods require the analyst to mathematically characterize the decision maker's preferences over a set of attributes in the form of a real-valued function. The resulting function, called a value or utility function, is then used to develop a cardinal ranking of the alternatives. That is, in the case where two alternatives are compared, preference-based methods can say that alternative A is preferred to B and also provide a measure of how much A is preferred to B, thus, providing a measure of the global preference of the decision maker.

There are two general types of preference functions that are based on utility theory. A preference representation function under certainty is called a value function, and a preference representation function under uncertainty is called a utility function. Both functions lead to a ranking of the alternatives and are described and illustrated below.

2.3.1 Multiattribute Value Functions

A multiattribute value (MAV) function can be used in decision situations where no uncertainty is involved. In other words, the outcomes of various actions or alternatives must be known with certainty in order for this approach to apply. Multiattribute value functions apply to the same type of decision problems as the scoring methods do (that is, multiattribute problems), but can also be used for solving multiple-objective programming problems. In fact, scoring methods can be thought of as a simple MAV model and, although often not stated explicitly, they require similar assumptions as a multiattribute value function.

In MAV function approaches, the quantification of a value function is central to developing a ranking of the alternatives. The value function v mathematically represents the decision maker's preferences over a set of alternatives X that is characterized by m attributes or objectives, represented by vector x. This value function assigns a number to each of the alternatives. The functional value of a value function is a measure of an alternative's "worthiness," and is quantified in terms of the decision maker's preferences. The alternatives are rank-ordered based on the magnitude of the value function, and the one with the highest functional value is selected as the most preferred.

2.3.1.1 The functional form of a value function.   A decision maker's preference and indifference between a pair of alternatives can be described mathematically using value functions. A decision maker is indifferent between two alternatives $x' = (x'_1, x'_2, \ldots, x'_m)$ and $x'' = (x''_1, x''_2, \ldots, x''_m)$ (that is, $x' \sim x''$) if and only if $v(x') = v(x'')$. A decision maker prefers alternative x' to x'' (that is, $x' \succ x''$) if and only if $v(x') > v(x'')$ (Evans, 1984).

The direct assessment of a value function, $v(x_1, x_2, \ldots, x_m)$, would be a very difficult task for the decision maker. It would require the decision maker to examine each alternative in terms of its attributes and then assign a value representing the degree of preference. For a large number of alternatives and attributes, this would be virtually impossible to do in an objective and consistent fashion. Thus, to accomplish the assessment of a multiattribute value function, $\nu_1(x_1, x_2, \ldots, x_m)$, the function is decomposed into m single-attribute functions, $\nu_i(x_i)$. The decision maker then assesses preferences for each alternative with respect to only one attribute at a time. As we will show, even the derivation of a value function for a single attribute, $\nu_i(x_i)$, can be difficult. The single-attribute approach, however, is much simpler than considering all attributes simultaneously.

Given that the assessment process has been decomposed in the above fashion, the question arises as to how to combine the single-attribute functions into an appropriate multiattribute value function, $\nu(x_1, \ldots, x_m) = f[\nu_1(x_1), \ldots, \nu_m(x_m)]$. In other words, one needs to determine the form of the function, f. One of the simplest ways to form a multiattribute value function is to develop a simple additive function that is a linear combination of the m individual functions. This function can be represented as

$$\nu(x_1, \ldots, x_m) = \alpha_1 \nu_1(x_1) + \ldots + \alpha_m \nu_m(x_m) \tag{2-2}$$

where α_i corresponds to the relative importance of attribute i, x_i is a measure of how an alternative performs in terms of attribute i, and $\nu_i(x_i)$ is the single-attribute value function of the ith attribute. Note that the relative importances are required to sum to one: $\sum_{i=1}^{m} \alpha_i = 1$.

Although the additive value function is the simplest way to combine the single-attribute value functions into a multiattribute value function, an important and somewhat restrictive requirement on a decision maker's preferences over pairs of attributes must be satisfied. This requirement is the *corresponding trade-offs condition* (Keeney and Raiffa, 1976). Two attributes, x_1 and x_2, satisfy the corresponding trade-offs condition if an increase of c in the value of x_2 is worth d units in x_1, regardless of the values of x_1, x_2, c, and d. If this condition holds, then, in the case of two attributes, the preference structure is additive.

In the case of three or more attributes, a condition called *mutual preferential independence* must hold in order for an additive preference structure to exist. Consider the case of three attributes, x_1, x_2, and x_3. The pair of attributes x_1 and x_2 is *preferentially independent* of x_3, if preferences for different values of attributes x_1 and x_2 do not depend on the level of attribute x_3. In order to understand the concept of preferential independence, suppose that the three attributes, x_1, x_2, and x_3 correspond to the time to complete a project, the project cost, and risk, respectively. Suppose that the decision maker is considering a pair of options and prefers the option with a completion time of 5 days at a cost of $100 over a second option of 10 days at a cost of $80 where both options have a risk of failure of 0.2. If the time to complete a project and the project cost are preferentially independent of risk, then the decision maker should still prefer the option with a completion time of 5 days, $100 option over the 10 days, $80 option at any other level of risk. If, by similar analysis, attributes $\{x_2, x_3\}$ are preferentially independent of attribute x_1, and attributes $\{x_1, x_3\}$ are preferentially independent of attribute x_2, then the three attributes, x_1, x_2, and x_3 are said to be *mutually preferentially independent*.

In the case of four or more attributes, every subset of attributes must be preferentially independent of its complement (that is, the remaining attributes) in order for the attributes to be mutually preferentially independent.

Mutual preferential independence often holds for attributes that have existing measurement scales associated with them. For example, the decision maker will often display mutual preferential independence when considering the cost of a car measured in dollars, the gas mileage measured in miles per gallon, and the noise level measured in decibels. It is when the attributes do not have an associated scale (for example, the appearance of the car and color preference), that mutual preferential independence may not hold.

In cases where the mutual preferential independence is not satisfied, the additive form for the value function should not be used, but one of many other types of value functions may be used instead. For example, one such form is the multiplicative decomposition

$$K\nu(x_1, x_2, \ldots, x_m) + 1 = [K\alpha_1\nu_1(x_1) + 1][K\alpha_2\nu_2(x_2) + 1] \ldots [K\alpha_m\nu_m(x_m) + 1] \qquad (2\text{-}3)$$

If we compare this to the additive function, we see that an additional scaling factor, K, must be assessed. When mutual preferential independence does not hold, then the weights on the attributes do not sum to one ($\sum_{i=1}^{m} \alpha_i \neq 1$). (Note that the multiplicative form reduces to the additive form if $\sum_{i=1}^{m} \alpha_i = 1$, in which case $K = 0$).

Other forms of the multiattribute value function are sometimes used when mutual preferential independence does not hold. These include, for example, the quasiadditive and multilinear forms. In all cases, the assessment of these functions is more difficult than the linear additive function because of the existence of additional factors. For a complete list of the various forms of a value function see Zeleny (1982).

2.3.1.2 Assessment of MAV functions.

The process of assessing the multiattribute value (MAV) function involves fairly detailed interviews between the decision maker and the analyst, and can be both difficult and time-consuming. Consider the assessment of an additive value function that involves the construction of m single-attribute value functions, $\nu_i(x_i)$. Here, the decision maker must assess the degree of preference over different levels of each attribute. Note that the value function associated with a given attribute may not be linear in shape. For example, suppose that reliability measured in terms of the probability that the system is operational over a given time period is an attribute used to differentiate between various alternative systems. A decision maker may strongly prefer high values of reliability and may want to avoid low values. In this case, the decision maker may not think that going from a reliability of 0.25 to 0.5 is the same as going from 0.5 to 0.75.

An approach that is widely used for constructing a single-attribute value function is called the mid-value splitting technique (Keeney and Raiffa, 1976). This method begins by asking the decision maker to determine the two values of a given attribute i,

x_i^L and x_i^U, that correspond to the lower and upper bounds of that attribute, respectively. Typically, the value function quantities assigned to these two points are $v_i(x_i^L) = 0$ and $v_i(x_i^U) = 1$. The decision maker is then asked to identify a point, $x_i^{0.5}$, at which he or she would feel just as good about moving from x_i^L to $x_i^{0.5}$ as about moving from $x_i^{0.5}$ to x_i^U. This point is assigned a value of 0.5 (that is, $v_i(x_i^{0.5}) = 0.5$). The process continues in the same manner to find $x_i^{0.25}$ and $x_i^{0.75}$. Once enough points have been identified, a curve can be fitted for $v_i(x_i)$. An example of a value function is illustrated in Figure 2.1.

A single-attribute value function for each of the m attributes is derived using the above process. Once all of the individual value functions have been derived, the weights, α_i, on the attributes must be determined. The attribute weights are assessed by asking the decision maker to select two points between which he or she is indifferent. For example, in the case of two attributes, the two points may be $x = (x_1, x_2)$ and $x' = (x'_1, x'_2)$. From the definition of indifference, we know the value functions should be equal at these two points [that is, $v(x_1, x_2) = v(x'_1, x'_2)$]. Using the additive form for the value function, we have that $\alpha_1 v_1(x_1) + \alpha_2 v_2(x_2) = \alpha_1 v_1(x'_1) + \alpha_2 v_2(x'_2)$. Because the single-attribute value functions have already been assessed, the values of $v_1(x_1)$, $v_2(x_2)$, $v_1(x'_1)$, $v_2(x'_2)$ are known. The only unknowns are the two attribute weights, α_1 and α_2. We also know that $\alpha_1 + \alpha_2 = 1$. Thus, one can solve the system of two equations in two unknowns to find α_1 and α_2. Of course, this procedure can be extended to more than two attributes. For m attributes, this would require the identification of $m - 1$ pairs of points where the decision maker is indifferent between each pair.

The single-attribute value functions are then aggregated into the overall value function, $v(x)$, using the assessed weights α_i ($i = 1, \ldots, m$). That is,

$$v(x) = v(x_1, x_2, \ldots, x_m) = \sum_{i=1}^{m} \alpha_i v_i(x_i) \qquad (2\text{-}4)$$

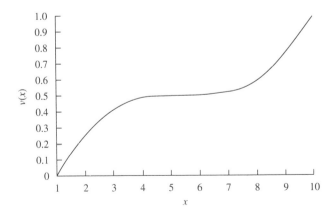

Figure 2.1   A Single-Attribute Value Function

2.3.1.3 Finding the best alternative.

Once the MAV function is obtained, the solution to the problem becomes trivial. With the multiattribute problem, where a finite set of n alternatives is evaluated with respect to a set of m attributes, the alternative that results in the highest value of the value function is selected.

However, in the case of a multiobjective problem, where an infinite set of alternatives must be evaluated, the optimization problem is solved using mathematical programming. In this case, alternatives are represented by various levels of the decision variables, x, and the m attributes are represented by m objective functions, $f_i(x)(i = 1, 2, \ldots, m)$. The corresponding mathematical programming problem can be stated as

$$\text{Maximize} \quad \nu[f_1(x), f_2(x), \ldots, f_m(x)]$$
$$\text{subject to} \quad x \in X \tag{2-5}$$

In other words, the multiobjective problem is solved as a single-objective problem through the evaluation of the value function (Evans, 1984). This single-objective problem can be solved using a mathematical programming approach such as the Simplex Method (in the case of linear value functions and linear constraints), quadratic programming, or other nonlinear search techniques. Note that the value function will very rarely be linear—this would only occur if each of the single-attribute value functions was also linear. The solution to Problem (2-5) will identify the alternative that results in the highest functional value of the value function.

2.3.1.4 Simple Multiattribute Rating Technique (SMART).

SMART, developed by Edwards (1977), is a simplified version of MAV function that has also been implemented in software. The SMART procedure includes the following steps:

1. Determine a value tree or objectives hierarchy.
2. Specify evaluation measures or attributes for each of the lowest-level elements of the hierarchy.
3. Determine a value function for each attribute. Note that this is a simplified version of the approach described in Section 2.3.1.2, where the value function is assumed to be linear.
4. Determine the weight for each single-attribute value function. Again, a simplified version of the approach described earlier is used (see Section 2.3.1.2). SMART uses swing weights, where each of the attributes is increased from its least preferred level to its most preferred level. From this, the decision maker determines which attribute is the most important, second most important, and so on, and also by how many times it is more important. These numbers are then normalized to sum to one.
5. Determine the score for each alternative with respect to each attribute (usually a linear value function is assumed) and use the linear additive value function to derive the overall rating for each alternative.

Decision makers seem to find the SMART approach simpler to implement than the original MAV function assessment.

2.3.1.5 A final note.   The analyst plays an important role in the process of assessing multiattribute value functions. He must ensure that the decision maker is aware of the underlying assumptions of the approach and must also ensure that the decision maker is consistent throughout the process. The analyst must also ensure that the decision maker understands the meaning and the purpose of the questions.

2.3.2 Multiattribute Utility Functions

Multiattribute utility theory (MAUT) is a methodology that aids the decision maker in selecting the best option from among a set of n alternatives in the presence of uncertainty. In other words, MAUT is used in situations where the decision outcomes are not known with certainty for a chosen action or alternative. Instead, the likelihood of the decision outcomes is described by probability density functions over the attribute space.

Central to the use of MAUT is the development of a multiattribute utility function, $u(x_1, x_2, \ldots, x_m)$. This function mathematically represents the decision maker's preferences over probability distributions defined on the attribute space. Because of the uncertainty involved in the problem, the expected value of this function is used to assign a number called the "expected utility" to each alternative. The expected utility is a measure of the "worthiness" of each alternative. The alternatives are ranked according to decreasing expected utilities, and the alternative with the highest expected utility is chosen as the most preferred.

2.3.2.1 Axioms of utility theory.   There are several axioms underlying utility theory that must be satisfied in order for the best decision to be consistent with the maximum expected utility. In addition, these axioms relate to the use of reference lotteries for quantifying a decision maker's preferences under uncertainty. These axioms are:

1. *Ordering of outcomes and transitivity*—For any two alternatives, the decision maker can establish either preference or indifference between the alternatives and the preference order is transitive. For example, the *transitivity* axiom states that if car A is preferred to car B, and car B is preferred to car C, then car A must be preferred to car C.

2. *Reduction of compound uncertain events*—The decision maker can always establish indifference between a complicated mixture of lotteries versus simple uncertain events. That is, complicated lotteries can always be reduced to simpler terms.

3. *Continuity*—The decision maker is indifferent between a certain outcome A and a lottery between two uncertain outcomes A_1, and A_2, where A lies between A_1 and A_2.

4. *Substitutability*—A decision maker is indifferent between an uncertain event that includes outcome A and a lottery that is formed by substituting an equivalent for A.

5. *Monotonicity*—Given two lotteries with the same outcomes, the decision maker always prefers the lottery with the higher probability of winning the preferred outcome.

6. *Invariance*—Only the payoffs and probabilities are needed to determine the decision maker's preferences among uncertain events.

7. *Boundedness*—No outcomes are considered infinitely bad or infinitely good.

See Clemen (1991) for a more detailed discussion of the above axioms, paradoxes, and their implications.

Given that the preceding axioms hold, the preferences among alternatives are defined in terms of the expected utilities. The decision maker is indifferent between two alternatives, $x' = (x'_1, x'_2, \ldots, x'_m)$ and $x'' = (x''_1, x''_2, \ldots, x''_m)$ (that is, $x' \sim x''$), if and only if $E[u(x')] = E[u(x'')]$. The decision maker prefers alternative x' to x'' (that is, $x' \succ x''$) if and only if $Eu[(x')] > E[u(x'')]$. Note that $E[u(x')]$ denotes the expected utility of alternative x'.

2.3.2.2 Use of lotteries in assessing MAUT functions.

The assessment of a multiattribute utility function is even more difficult than the assessment of a multiattribute value function because lotteries are used to address the uncertainty present in the problem when using MAUT. However, a major advantage of the MAUT function over the MAV function is its ability to explicitly take into account the uncertainty in the decision outcomes. In many decision situations, it is not possible to say with certainty what will occur when a particular course of action is chosen. For example, a heart patient may have a number of courses of action to choose from, including open heart surgery, angioplasty, or doing nothing. However, the outcome of each of these options is not known with certainty. The quantification of a MAUT function will allow the patient to determine which course of action would lead to the best expected outcome.

As with value functions, the assessment of a utility function is usually accomplished by decomposing the multiattribute function into m single-attribute functions. The component (single-attribute) utility functions, $u_i(x_i)$, are constructed through detailed interviews with the decision maker. Because the outcomes of decisions are uncertain, the decision maker is presented with lotteries in order to quantify his or her utility over the given attribute. For the purposes of discussion, suppose the attribute under consideration is money. The value of money is not viewed the same by all individuals—both the level of wealth and the attitude toward risk can influence a decision maker's preferences.

The following illustration is derived from Goicoechea et al. (1982). Consider two investors faced with the same two investment alternatives. The first investment alternative requires an initial outlay of $50,000 and will result in a gain of $200,000 with a

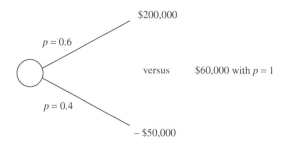

Figure 2.2   Example of Two Lotteries

probability of 0.6, or a loss of $50,000 with a probability of 0.4. The expected gain from this lottery is $100,000. The second investment alternative also involves an outlay of $50,000 but has a certain gain of $60,000. (See Figure 2.2.)

Now consider the wealth of the two investors. Suppose that the two investors have a total wealth of $50,000 and $1,000,000, respectively. The first investor would likely choose not to invest in the risky alternative (the first alternative) because there is a fairly high likelihood that he could lose his entire wealth. However, the second investor may be willing to take the chance of losing a small percentage of her total wealth by taking the risky alternative. With this alternative, there is a fairly good chance that she may receive a fairly attractive return.

The behavior displayed by the first investor is called risk-aversion. A person is *risk-averse* when he or she prefers a certain (that is, with a probability of 1) gain over a larger, but uncertain expected gain. In the above example, the certain gain of $60,000 is preferred by the first investor to the uncertain expected gain of $100,000.

The assessment process used for utility functions requires the decision maker to establish a *certainty equivalent* (CE) to a lottery. A certainty equivalent to a given lottery is a certain amount CE, where the decision maker is indifferent between CE and the lottery. For example, consider the lottery on the left in Figure 2.2. One decision maker may give a certainty equivalent of, say, $80,000, whereas a second decision maker may give a value of CE = $120,000. The attitude of the first decision maker is *risk-averse* because his certainty equivalent is less than the expected value of the gamble ($100,000). The attitude of the second decision maker is that of a *risk-taker or risk-preferrer* because her CE is greater than the expected value of $100,000. When the certainty equivalent is equal to the expected value, then the decision maker's attitude is *risk-neutral*.

2.3.2.3 Functional forms of MAUT functions.

One of the fundamental concepts in MAUT is *utility independence* (Keeney and Raiffa, 1976). An attribute, x_1, is utility-independent of attribute x_2 if preferences for uncertain scenarios (lotteries) involving different levels of x_1 are independent of the value of x_2. In other words, if at a given level of x_2 the certainty equivalent is equal to c for a lottery involving equal chances for the best and the worst values of attribute x_1, then the certainty equivalent

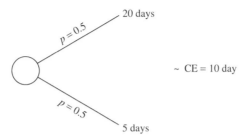

20 days

$p = 0.5$

~ CE = 10 day

$p = 0.5$

5 days

Figure 2.3   Lotteries for Project Completion Example

should remain at c regardless of the value of x_2. For example, suppose that the best and the worst values for the completion of a project are 5 days and 20 days, respectively. Moreover, the decision maker has assessed a certainty equivalent equal to 10 days for the lottery involving 5 and 20 days at a fifty-fifty-percent chance. This situation is shown in Figure 2.3. Project completion time is utility-independent of cost, then, if the decision maker's certainty equivalent remains at 10 days regardless of the project cost. If x_2 is also utility-independent of x_1, then x_1 and x_2 are said to be mutually utility-independent. In general, a subset of attributes, y, is mutually independent of the set of attributes x if y is utility-independent of x for all possible attributes y. That is, with n attributes, in order to test the utility independence of every possible subset, one has to perform $2^n - 2$ tests (Bunn, 1984). Fortunately, in practice, fewer tests are required. It can be shown that attributes are mutually utility-independent if and only if attribute x is utility-independent and is preferentially independent (refer to Section 2.3.1.1 for the definition of preferential independence) of each of the remaining attributes (Keeney and Raiffa, 1976). Various utility-independence conditions imply specific forms of utility functions. However, only the additive and multiplicative forms are generally used in practice. The additive utility function can be represented as

$$u(x_1, \ldots, x_m) = k_1 u_1(x_1) + \ldots + k_m u_m(x_m) \tag{2-6}$$

where $u(x_1, \ldots, x_m)$ is on a scale from 0 to 1, the component utility functions $u_i(x_i)$ are on a scale from 0 to 1, and the scaling constants k_i are positive and sum to one. The multiplicative form is given as

$$1 + ku(x_1, \ldots, x_m) = \prod_{i=1}^{m} [1 + kk_i u_i(x_i)] \tag{2-7}$$

where again $u(x_1, \ldots, x_m)$ is on a scale from 0 to 1 and the component utility functions $u_i(x_i)$ are on a scale from 0 to 1. However, the scaling constants k_i may be greater or less than one, and the constant k is chosen to satisfy Equation (2-8):

$$1 + k = \prod_{i=1}^{m} [1 + kk_i] \tag{2-8}$$

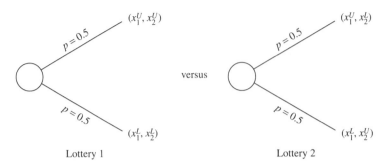

versus

Lottery 1   Lottery 2

Figure 2.4   Lotteries Used in Determining the Form of the Utility
Function

In order to decide whether to use the additive or multiplicative form for the multiattribute utility function, two lotteries are presented to the decision maker. For instance, in the case of 2 attributes i and j, let x_i^U and x_i^L correspond to the most desirable and least desirable values for attribute i and let x_j^U and x_j^L be the most desirable and least desirable values for attribute j. Note that higher values of attributes i and j are assumed to be preferred to lower values. Lottery one involves a fifty-fifty chance of getting either the best or the worst values of the two attributes i and j, whereas the second lottery involves a fifty-fifty chance of getting the best of one attribute and the worst of the other. This is depicted in Figure 2.4.

If the decision maker is indifferent between lotteries 1 and 2 for all pairs of attributes, then the additive form holds, in which case the scaling constants are positive and sum to one. If lottery 2 is preferred for all pairs of attributes, or if lottery 1 is preferred on all pairs of attributes, then this (along with preferential independence and utility independence) implies that the multiplicative form is appropriate for use. When lottery 2 is preferred to lottery 1, the decision maker is multiattribute risk-averse, and $-1 < k < 0$. If lottery 1 is preferred to lottery 2, then the decision maker is consistently a risk-seeker and $k > 0$. If lottery 1 is preferred for only some pairs of attributes, then the contradiction must be resolved (Bunn, 1984; Goicoechea et al., 1982).

2.3.2.4 Assessment of MAUT functions.
The assessment of an additive or multiplicative utility function requires the assessment of m component (single-attribute) utility functions. The shape of the curve defined by a given component utility function is determined by the risk attitude of the decision maker (see Figure 2.5). For a risk-averse decision maker, the utility curve is curved and opening downward (concave). A risk-neutral decision maker has a straight-line utility curve. And, for a risk-seeker, the utility curve is curved and opening upward.

In order to assess a component utility function, various points on the curve are determined by the decision maker using the following procedure. Consider the assessment of the component utility function, $u_i(x_i)$, for a particular attribute x_i. The

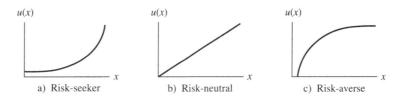

Figure 2.5 Shapes of Utility Curves

first step is to choose two values of the given attribute i, x_i^L and x_i^U, that correspond to lowest (worst) and highest (best) values of the ith attribute, respectively. The following utilities are assigned to these two values: $u_i(x_i^L) = 0$ and $u_i(x_i^u) = 1.0$. The decision maker is then told that he or she has a probability $(1 - p)$ of getting x_i^L and a probability of p of getting x_i^U. The decision maker is then asked, "What least amount x would you accept for certain instead of taking the gamble?" In other words, the decision maker is asked to give his or her certainty equivalent for the lottery shown in Figure 2.6.

Once x (the certainty equivalent) has been specified by the decision maker, the utility of x is set equal to p (that is, $u_i(x) = p$). To show this mathematically, note that because the decision maker is indifferent between the lottery and the specified value x, the following relationship must hold:

$$pu_i(x_i^U) + (1 - p)u_i(x_i^L) = 1.0u_i(x) \tag{2-9}$$

Since $u_i(x_i^L) = 0$ and $u_i(x_i^U) = 1.0$, Equation (2-9) leads to $p = u_i(x)$.

Additional points on the utility curve can be found by changing the value of p in the preceding lottery. Typically, p is chosen to be 0.5, 0.25, and 0.75 in order to construct three points (in addition to the two anchoring points, x_i^L and x_i^U) on the utility curve for the given attribute. An assumed exponential function can then be fitted to the points.

After the component utility functions have been assessed, the scaling constants in Equations (2-6) or (2-7) must be determined. The scaling constants, k_i, which represent the relative importance of the attributes, can be assessed using the following process.

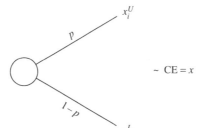

Figure 2.6 Lotteries Used for Assessing a Single-Attribute Utility Function.

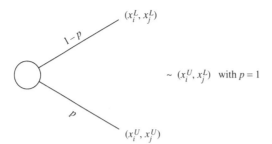

Figure 2.7 Lotteries Used for Assessing the Scaling Constants

The decision maker first chooses an attribute against which the other attributes will be compared. Suppose that the ith attribute is chosen. In order to compare another attribute, say, attribute j, with the ith attribute, the decision maker is presented with the following two alternatives: The first alternative has the ith attribute at its best value and all of the remaining attributes at their worst values [that is, (x_i^U, x_j^L)]. The second alternative has all of the attributes at their worst values [that is, (x_i^L, x_j^L)]. The level of jth attribute in the second alternative is improved until the decision maker is indifferent between the two alternatives. Suppose that x_j^P represents this particular level of attribute j. Because the utilities of the two alternatives are equal at this point, the values of the scaling constants for attributes i and j are related as follows:

$$k_i - k_j u_j(x_j^P) = 0 \qquad (2\text{-}10)$$

By comparing the ith attribute with each of the remaining attributes, this procedure can be used to generate $(m-1)$ indifference pairs [that is, $(m-1)$ nonlinear equations in m unknowns are constructed]. An additional equation can be obtained by asking the decision maker to decide on the probability p that would make him indifferent between the lottery (x_i^U, x_j^U) with probability p, and (x_i^L, x_j^L) with probability $(1-p)$ and the alternative (x_i^U, x_j^L) with certainty. (See Figure 2.7.) This gives m nonlinear equations in m unknowns that can now be solved to get the values of the scaling constants, k_i. The component utility functions and scaling constants can be used in Equations (2.2) or (2.3) to obtain the overall utility function.

2.3.2.5 Finding the best alternative.
Once the multiattribute utility function $u(x)$ has been assessed, the alternatives can be ranked. The assessed utility function $u(x)$ and a set of conditional probability density functions $\{ f_i(x_i) \}$ for an alternative x are used to compute the expected utility for that alternative as follows:

$$E[u(x)] = \int_{-\infty}^{\infty} u(x) f(x)\, dx \qquad (2\text{-}11)$$

(Note that $f(x)$ can be computed as the product of the conditional density functions if the attributes are probabilistically independent.) The alternative with the highest expected utility is the highest ranking alternative.

2.3.3 Summary

As should be apparent in this brief overview of the preference-based approaches (that is, MAV and MAUT functions) there are a number of practical difficulties with these methods. The assessment of the component value and utility functions requires information that is difficult for the decision maker to provide, and this precludes their widespread use. For example, French (1984) argues against using the value function and the utility function because the decision maker is almost always asked to make hypothetical choices between alternatives that may have no practical reality. Recall that in order to calculate the weights, α_i, the decision maker is asked to select two points (x_1, x_2) and (x'_1, x'_2) between which he is indifferent. In reality, these two points may not be part of the alternative set.

Additional difficulties are encountered in assessing scaling constants for MAV and MAUT functions and in ensuring that the underlying assumptions (for example, preferential independence and utility independence) are satisfied. In MAUT, the inclusion of uncertainty results in additional complexities in both the assessment and computational processes. The reader is referred to Goicoechea et al. (1982) for additional discussion on these difficulties. Because of the reasons stated above, other approaches have been developed that require less cognitive burden on the decision maker. In the sections that follow, we describe and illustrate three such methods—the analytic hierarchy process, outranking methods, and goal programming.

Note that, in spite of the difficulties encountered in using MAV and MAUT functions, these approaches remain a benchmark for multiattribute decision methods because of their strong theoretical foundations. Moreover, MAUT is one of the few approaches that can incorporate uncertainty in the process, whereas none of the simpler methods described in the following sections can accommodate uncertainty directly.

2.4 The Analytic Hierarchy Process

The analytic hierarchy process (AHP) is a multicriteria decision-making technique that allows the consideration of both objective and subjective factors in selecting the best alternative. This approach is used to arrive at a ratio-scale cardinal ranking of alternatives for multiattribute decision problems. AHP was originally introduced by Thomas Saaty in the mid 1970s (Saaty, 1977, 1980, 1994). Since its development, AHP has been applied in a wide variety of practical applications, including those related to economics and planning, energy policy, health, conflict resolution, project selection, and budget allocation (see Zahedi, 1986; Golden et al., 1989). In fact, AHP is one of the most popular multicriteria decision-making methodologies available today. Its popularity is due to its flexibility and ease of use, as well as the availability of a software package called Expert Choice (Decision Support Software, Inc., 1986).

The analytic hierarchy process is based on three principles: decomposition, comparative judgments, and synthesis of priorities. The *decomposition principle* requires that the decision problem be decomposed into a hierarchy that captures the important elements of the problem. Higher elements in the hierarchy are more general goals and objectives, lower elements in the hierarchy are more specific attributes, and the lowest level are the alternatives. Each level must be linked to the next-higher level, and adjacent elements within one level must not be too disparate (so that they can be compared using a common relative-importance scale). The *principle of comparative judgments* requires assessments of pairwise comparisons (on a scale of relative importance) of the elements within a given level, with respect to their parent in the next-higher level. These assessments are collected into comparison matrices where each entry in the matrix belongs to the relative-importance scale used in the comparisons. The entries in the matrix are then used to generate a derived ratio scale that reflects the local priorities of the elements in the hierarchy. The *synthesis of priorities principle* takes each of the derived ratio-scale local priorities in the various levels of the hierarchy and constructs a composite (global) set of priorities for the elements at the lowest level of the hierarchy (that is, the alternatives).

The underlying theory that supports the use of AHP is based on four axioms. These axioms relate to (1) the scale that is used in performing the pairwise comparisons (the scale is reciprocal in nature), (2) the necessity for the homogeneity of the elements being compared (so that there is an upper bound on the scale and the same scale can be used in all comparisons), (3) independence and dependence requirements among various elements and levels within the hierarchy (to allow an additive approach to be used in synthesizing the local priorities), and (4) the completeness of the hierarchy (that is, all criteria and all alternatives have been included in the hierarchy). More specifically, the axioms are as follows (for more details, see Saaty, 1986):

1. *Reciprocal*—Whenever paired comparisons of alternatives or attributes are made, both members of the pair must be judged on a relative scale. That is, if A is judged to be 5 times more preferred to B, then B is automatically 1/5 preferred to A.

2. *Homogeneity* (*Bounded Preference*)—To ensure consistency, the attributes or alternatives must be of the same order of magnitude with respect to the basis of comparison. For example, if we are comparing two jobs in terms of the salary level, then we should not compare the two jobs if the preference between salary levels is widely different. If job A pays $200,000 and job B pays $10,000, then job A will be infinitely preferred to job B. When the attributes or alternatives are widely disparate, it should be possible to aggregate them into homogeneous groups. When this is done, the clusters can be compared instead of the individual elements.

3. *Hierarchic Composition*—Consider a hierarchy with several levels. Decomposition of elements into a hierarchy requires that smaller (more detailed) elements be clustered below a higher-level goal. This means that each of the lower-level ele-

ments must depend on the "outer" parent to which they belong. The elements within a level may also depend on one another (inner dependence) with respect to a property in another level. For example, there might be an input-output relationship among elements in one level with respect to a higher-level goal, say productivity evaluation. In order to relate (compare) elements within a given level of the hierarchy with respect to the parent element above, the following dependence relationships must hold: (a) the lower-level elements must be outer-dependent on the associated level above, (b) the lower level must not be inner-dependent with respect to the elements in the level above, and (c) the higher level must not be outer-dependent on the level below. If the above "dependence" requirements are satisfied, then the problem can be decomposed into hierarchy and the additive synthesis process can be used.

In some cases the above requirements are not satisfied. For example, the priorities on the criteria may depend on the set of alternatives, priorities of higher-order criteria may depend on lower-level criteria, or an alternative may depend on other alternatives. A hierarchy is not appropriate in this case, and the standard AHP evaluation and synthesis process should not be used. Note that the AHP has been generalized to accommodate these types of dependencies. The problem, in this case, is described as a network with feedback instead of as a hierarchy, and the so-called "supermatrix" approach is used in the evaluation and synthesis process (for more details see Saaty, 1994 and 1996).

4. *Expectations*—Expectations are the beliefs about the rank of alternatives derived from the prior knowledge of the decision maker. This axiom requires that the decision maker specify the problem elements adequately in order for the outcome to match these expectations. That is, all of the essential alternatives, dependencies, and criteria must be represented in the hierarchy in order for the ranking to match the expectations.

See Saaty (1986, 1994) for a more detailed discussion of the axioms and their consequences.

The analytic hierarchy process begins with the identification of the criteria (attributes) to be used in the evaluation of alternatives. These criteria must then be organized in a hierarchical structure. For a discussion on the development and structuring of criteria, see Chapter 1. Each level of the hierarchy consists of a few criteria, and each criterion is, in turn, decomposed into subcriteria. The process continues down to the most specific elements of the problem, typically the decision alternatives, which are listed at the bottom of the hierarchy.

Once the hierarchy has been constructed, the relative importance or priority of each of the elements (such as criteria, subcriteria, and alternatives) must be determined. This is achieved through a pairwise comparison of the elements with respect to the element directly above. In general, this comparison takes the form: "How important is element 1 when compared to element 2 with respect to the element above?" The decision maker would then provide one of the following responses in either numeric or linguistic fashion:

Importance	Numerical Rating*
Equally Important (preferred, likely)	1
Moderately Important	3
Strongly Important	5
Very Strongly Important	7
Extremely Important	9

*2, 4, 6, 8 are intermediate values.

The responses to the pairwise comparisons at each level of the hierarchy are placed into a comparison matrix. For example, a problem that has four criteria and five alternatives would have five separate comparison matrices, one for the pairwise comparisons of the criteria and one each for the pairwise comparisons of the alternatives with respect to each of the four criteria.

The matrix in Figure 2.8 corresponds to the form of a pairwise comparison matrix between five alternatives with respect to a given criterion. The numbers (on a scale of 1 to 9) correspond to ratio scales. That is, a value of 7 for a_{24} in the above table means that alternative 2 is 7 times more preferred to alternative 4 with respect to the given criterion. Note further that the preference ratio of alternative 4 to alternative 2 would then be 1/7. The local priorities (priorities on the criteria, subcriteria, and alternatives) are determined by calculating the normalized principal right eigenvector (that is, the eigenvector with the largest eigenvalue) corresponding to each of the comparison matrices. The local priorities at each level of the hierarchy are then "synthesized" using a weighted sum to determine the cardinal ranking of the alternatives.

The computation of the principal right eigenvector can be difficult to perform without the use of appropriate software. Methods using simple procedures such as column sums, row sums, averaging, and normalization have been developed to allow the user

	Alt 1	Alt 2	Alt 3	Alt 4	Alt 5
Alt 1	1	a_{12}	a_{13}	a_{14}	a_{15}
Alt 2	$1/a_{12}$	1	a_{23}	a_{24}	a_{25}
Alt 3	$1/a_{13}$	$1/a_{23}$	1	a_{34}	a_{35}
Alt 4	$1/a_{14}$	$1/a_{24}$	$1/a_{34}$	1	a_{45}
Alt 5	$1/a_{15}$	$1/a_{25}$	$1/a_{35}$	$1/a_{45}$	1

Figure 2.8   Pairwise Comparison Matrix Used in AHP

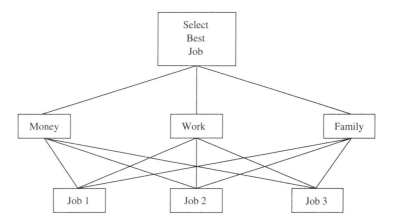

Figure 2.9   Complete Hierarchy for the Career Choice Problem

to approximate the principal eigenvector. This procedure is illustrated in the example that follows.

Consider an engineer who is deciding among three different jobs. Her preferences are expressed in terms of three different attributes: the amount of money she will make, the type of work she will be performing, and family considerations. The hierarchy shown in Figure 2.9 corresponds to this decision problem.

Suppose that she assesses the following preferences among the attributes

"Money is between 'of equal importance to' and 'of moderately more importance than' the type of work,"
"Family and work are equally important," and
"Family is moderately more important than money."

The comparison matrix in Figure 2.10 summarizes the results. The engineer's pairwise evaluations of the three jobs with respect to each of the three attributes—money, type of work, and family considerations—are summarized in Figures 2.11–2.13.

The principal eigenvector associated with each comparison matrix is then computed and normalized to determine the local priority weights. The approximate method for the first comparison matrix is demonstrated in Table 2.4. In this approximate method, the column sums are computed first. Then the elements within each column of the comparison matrix are normalized by dividing each entry by its corresponding column sum. Finally, the row elements (which are now the new normalized values) are averaged to obtain an estimate for the relative importance of each criterion (money, type of work, and family considerations) (see Table 2.4). Table 2.5 shows the local priorities generated by using this process on the three remaining comparison matrices.

The final weights for each alternative are synthesized by multiplying the criteria weights shown in the last column of Table 2.4 by the local priorities of the alternatives

With respect to the overall goal, by how much is attribute i preferred to attribute j?

	Money	Work	Family
Money	1	2	1/3
Work	1/2	1	1
Family	3	1	1

Figure 2.10 Pairwise Comparison Matrix for the Criteria

With respect to amount of salary received, by how much is job i preferred to job j?

MONEY	Job A	Job B	Job C
Job A	1	4	7
Job B	1/4	1	2
Job C	1/7	1/2	1

Figure 2.11 Pairwise Comparison Matrix for the Jobs with Respect to Money*

given in each row of Table 2.5. For example, the final ranking of job A, V_A, is computed as

$$V_A = (0.288 \times 0.715) + (0.263 \times 0.263) + (0.449 \times 0.595)$$

$$V_A = 0.542$$

The resulting priorities for the three alternatives are shown in Table 2.6. From this table, the conclusion is that job A is the preferred alternative.

One of the important features of AHP is its ability to provide a measure for the consistency of the decision maker's judgment. In fact, none of the other commonly used approaches to solving multiattribute decision problems provide the ability for such consistency checks. As an example, consider the following situation: If a decision maker says that factor 1 is strongly more important than factor 2 and factor 2 is equally important to factor 3, then one would expect him or her to say that factor 1 is strongly more important than factor 3. If, for example, the decision maker says that factor 3 is more important than factor 1, then he or she is being inconsistent. AHP measures this

With respect to type of work, by how much is job i preferred to job j?

WORK	Job A	Job B	Job C
Job A	1	1/2	1
Job B	2	1	1/3
Job C	1	3	1

Figure 2.12 Pairwise Comparison Matrix for the Jobs with Respect to Work

With respect to family considerations, by how much is job i preferred to job j?

FAMILY	Job A	Job B	Job C
Job A	1	2	5
Job B	1/2	1	2
Job C	1/5	1/2	1

Figure 2.13 Pairwise Comparison Matrix for the Jobs with Respect to Family

---

*Note that because money is an objective measure, the actual dollars could be used rather than assessing the preferences (as shown in Figure 2.11). Note also that if the dollar values are used, the assumption of linear utility is required.

Table 2.4 Computations Required to Obtain the Local Priorities

	Money	Work	Family	Column entries divided by corresponding column sums			Row sums of last 3 columns	Weights
Money	1	2	1/3	0.222	0.5	0.1428	0.8648	0.288
Work	1/2	1	1	0.111	0.25	0.4286	0.7896	0.263
Family	3	1	1	0.666	0.25	0.4286	1.3446	0.449
Column sum	4.5	4	2.33					

inconsistency through the use of the consistency ratio, C.R., which is a function of the following three factors: (a) the dimension of the comparison matrix ($N \times N$), (b) a random index (R.I.), and (c) the dominant eigenvalue (λ_{max}):

$$C.R. = \frac{\lambda_{max} - N}{(N-1)(R.I.)} \qquad (2\text{-}12)$$

Random indices (R.I.) for various matrix sizes (N) have been approximated by Saaty (1980) based on simulation runs, as shown in Table 2.7. Generally, a consistency ratio of less than 0.1 is considered acceptable.

For the preceding example, the dominant eigenvalue for the job comparison matrix associated with the work attribute is approximately given by $\lambda_{max} = 3.371$. This was computed as follows: First, the matrix of pairwise comparisons is multiplied by the corresponding vector of priority weights (from Figure 2.12 and Table 2.5):

$$\begin{bmatrix} 1 & 0.5 & 1 \\ 2 & 1 & 0.33 \\ 1 & 3 & 1 \end{bmatrix} \times \begin{bmatrix} 0.263 \\ 0.288 \\ 0.449 \end{bmatrix} = \begin{bmatrix} 0.856 \\ 0.964 \\ 1.576 \end{bmatrix}$$

Table 2.5 Local Priorities of the Alternatives with Respect to Each Criterion

Alternatives	Local priorities (principal eigenvectors) shown as columns in this table		
	Money	Work	Family
Job A	0.715	0.263	0.595
Job B	0.187	0.288	0.277
Job C	0.098	0.449	0.128

Table 2.6 Global Priorities of the Alternatives

Alternative	Alternatives weighted by attribute weights
Job A	0.542
Job B	0.254
Job C	0.204

Table 2.7 Random Indices for Computing the Consistency Ratios

N	1	2	3	4	5	6	7	8	9	10	11	. . .
R.I.	0.00	0.00	0.58	0.90	1.12	1.24	1.32	1.41	1.45	1.49	1.51	. . .

The resulting vector is then divided by its corresponding vector of priority weights:

$$D = \begin{bmatrix} \dfrac{0.856}{0.263} & \dfrac{0.964}{0.288} & \dfrac{1.576}{0.449} \end{bmatrix}$$

$$D = \begin{bmatrix} 3.255 & 3.347 & 3.510 \end{bmatrix}$$

The dominant eigenvalue (λ_{max}) is computed by averaging the elements in vector D:

$$\lambda_{max} = (3.255 + 3.347 + 3.510) / 3 = 3.371$$

Finally, from Equation (2-12) the corresponding consistency ratio is given by

$$C.R. = \frac{3.371 - 3}{(2)(0.58)} = 0.007$$

Note that the value of 0.58 is the random index (R.I.) corresponding to three attributes. The value of C.R. = 0.007 indicates that the decision maker has been highly consistent in his or her assessments. However, two of the consistency ratios for the preceding example were equal to 0.320. For example, examine the comparison matrix in Figure 2.10. We see that the decision maker said that money is more important than type of work and that the type of work is equally as important as family. If consistent, the decision maker should say that money is more important than family; however, we see the statement that family was more important than money. Clearly, the decision maker's responses are inconsistent. Because the C.R. is much larger than the generally accepted value of 0.1, the decision maker should perform the pairwise comparison again. Note, however, that the decision maker does not have to be completely consistent (that is, C.R. = 0 is not required) in order for this approach to work.

Despite the widespread use of the analytic hierarchy process, this approach has not been without criticism. One of the main criticisms relates to what is called "rank reversal" (see Belton and Gear, 1983; Dyer, 1990; and Saaty, 1987). Rank reversal refers to the reversal of the preference order of the alternatives when new options are introduced in the problem. That is, the result of the analysis using AHP may indicate that alternative A is preferred to alternative B when alternative C is not being considered; but when alternative C is included as an option, it may indicate that alternative B is preferred to alternative A. This problem was first reported by Belton and Gear (1983), who proposed a modification to Saaty's conventional AHP. Schoner and Wedley (1989) also proposed an approach called the "referenced AHP" and compared it to the Belton and Gear "B-G modified AHP." They concluded that both approaches eliminate the rank reversal problem.

Other major criticisms about the AHP include (1) the ambiguity in the meaning of the relative importance of one factor when it is compared to another factor, and (2) the use of a 1-to-9 scale. Researchers such as Watson and Freeling (1982), Belton (1986), Dyer (1990), and Belton and Gear (1983) argue that the type of questions asked during the process of pairwise comparisons are meaningless. They argue that when the decision maker is asked to answer questions such as, How strongly do you prefer criterion A to criterion B? he or she must be clear about how much of criterion A (such as cost) is being compared to how much of criterion B (quality). The assumption here is that the decision maker must be thinking of some average quantities; otherwise, he or she would not be able to make a reasonable judgment (Boucher and MacStravic, 1991).

In spite of the above criticisms, AHP remains one of the most widely used multiattribute approaches. This is evident from the proliferation of articles published in refereed journals and presented at conferences. For more information on AHP, see Saaty (1980, 1987, 1994), Golden et al. (1989), and Zahedi (1986).

2.5 Outranking Methods

Multiattribute decision problems can also be analyzed through the use of outranking methods. These approaches, in general, require less information from the decision maker, information that also is easier to obtain than it is from the previously described methods. Outranking methods are a class of multicriteria decision-making techniques that provide an ordinal ranking (and sometimes only a partial ordering) of the alternatives. That is, in the case where two alternatives are compared, these approaches can only express that alternative A is preferred to alternative B, but cannot indicate by how much. This is the main disadvantage of these approaches. In this section, we describe and illustrate the ELECTRE I method. Several modifications of the ELECTRE I method (for example, ELECTRE II and III) and the Promethede method also fall under the category of outranking methods.

2.5.1 ELECTRE I

ELECTRE I allows the decision maker to choose the alternatives that are preferred for most of the criteria and that do not cause an unacceptable level of any one criterion. This is a procedure that is particularly suitable for a discrete set of alternatives (that is, a multiattribute problem). It examines the nondominated alternatives and searches for a subset of the nondominated solutions for which a certain degree of dissension or discord is acceptable by the decision maker. For example, an alternative i is included in the subset if it is preferred to alternative j from almost every viewpoint (that is, for almost all of the objectives or attributes). The construction of this subset is developed by defining an outranking relationship that captures the preferences of the decision maker. Preference relationships between the ith and jth alternatives are established for each criterion. These preference relations are then synthesized for each alternative to produce the outranking relationship. This relationship is then used to form a graph in which each node of the graph represents a nondominated alternative. This graph is then used to determine which of the alternatives is preferred.

The key concepts used in ELECTRE I are concordance, discordance, and threshold values. Before defining these concepts, we need to establish some notation. Let I represent the set of m criteria and let $w(k)$ be the weight on criterion k. The weights reflect the decision maker's preference structure and are elicited from the decision maker. The criterion that is considered to be the most important receives the highest weight, the next most important receives the next-highest weight, and so on.

The concordance between any two alternatives i and j is a weighted measure of the number of criteria for which alternative i is preferred or equal to alternative j. Mathematically, the concordance between alternatives i and j can be expressed by the ratio in Equation (2-13):

$$c(i, j) = \frac{\sum_{k \in A(i,j)} w(k) + (0.5) \sum_{k \in B(i,j)} w(k)}{\sum_k w(k)} \tag{2-13}$$

where $w(k)$ is the weight on criterion k, the set $A(i, j)$ contains the indices of the criteria for which alternative i is preferred to alternative j, and the set $B(i, j)$ contains the indices of the criteria for which alternative i is equally preferred to alternative j. The concordance indices are then summarized in a matrix C, where the entry $c(i, j)$ corresponds to the concordance between alternatives i and j.

The discord index is then defined for each pair of alternatives. In order to accomplish this, an interval scale is first constructed across all of the criteria. The goal is to assess the discomfort caused by improving one objective by a given interval at the expense of making another objective worse by a particular amount. The interval scale is obtained by assigning a certain number of points (out of a maximum of 100) to every criterion (the choice of 100 is arbitrary, and any other number will work equally well). The choice of the number of points to assign to each criterion is based on the level of importance (discomfort) that the decision maker wishes to attach to the range between the best and worst levels of the criterion. That is, the higher the point assignment, the greater the possible discomfort caused by going from the best to the worst value of the given objective. After assigning the interval scale to every criterion, the discord index between alternative i and j defined in Equation (2-14) is computed:

$$d(i, j) = \frac{\text{maximum interval where } j \text{ is preferred to } i}{100} \tag{2-14}$$

The concordance and discordance indices are then synthesized in order to define the outranking relation. Specifically, a graph of the relationships among the alternatives

Table 2.8 Criteria Ratings Used in
ELECTRE I Example

Criteria	Possible ratings
Price	15K, 20K, 25K, 30K
MPG	High, Medium, Low
Appearance	Great, Acceptable
Performance	Fast, Moderate

is constructed where alternative i is preferred to j (that is, an arc goes from i to j in the graph) if and only if

$$c(i, j) \geq p \qquad \text{and} \qquad d(i, j) \leq q$$

where p represents the minimal acceptable concordance and q represents the maximum discordance allowed. From this graph, the preferred alternatives can be determined. The results may be sensitive to the pair of threshold values, p and q, used above. The following example helps to illustrate the method.

Suppose that a decision maker wants to choose from among a group of alternative cars. There are four criteria upon which the decision maker intends to base her decision: price of the car, gas mileage, appearance, and performance. Table 2.8 summarizes these criteria and the rating scales established by the decision maker. The decision maker has rated four different cars on the basis of the criteria in Table 2.8; the results are summarized in Table 2.9.

The criteria have been assessed by the decision maker to have the following weights:

Criteria	Weights
Price	10
MPG	2
Appearance	6
Performance	2

The computation of the concordance index [see Equation (2-13)] between cars 1 and 2 is illustrated below; the complete concordance matrix appears in Table 2.10.

$$c(1, 2) = \frac{0 + 0 + 6 + (0.5)(2)}{20} = 0.35$$

Note that in developing the concordance matrix in Table 2.10, only the criteria weights were required as inputs from the decision maker.

Table 2.9 Ratings of Alternatives with Respect to Criteria

Criteria	Car 1	Car 2	Car 3	Car 4
Price	30K	25K	20K	15K
MPG	Low	Medium	Medium	High
Appearance	Great	Acceptable	Great	Acceptable
Performance	Fast	Fast	Moderate	Moderate

The criteria were then assigned the following maximum scale intervals by the decision maker in preparation for developing the discordance matrix:

Criteria	Discordance Index (Interval Scale)
Price	100
MPG	30
Appearance	60
Performance	40

The original assessments of the criteria were then translated using the preceding scales into the values summarized in Table 2.11. For example, for the price criterion there were four price categories and the maximum scale interval was 100. Thus, each improvement in the price is assigned 25 points (100/4). For the MPG criterion there were three MPG ratings and the maximum scale interval was 30. Thus, each improvement in gas mileage is assigned 10 points (30/3).

The discord index $d(i, j)$ is computed from Equation (2-14) for all criteria where j is preferred to i. Thus, when computing $d(1, 2)$ for cars 1 and 2, car 2 is preferred to car 1 in terms of price and MPG, as seen in the following equation:

Table 2.10 Concordance Matrix for ELECTRE I Example

	Car 1	Car 2	Car 3	Car 4
Car 1	—	0.35	0.25	0.4
Car 2	0.65	—	0.15	0.25
Car 3	0.75	0.85	—	0.35
Car 4	0.6	0.75	0.65	—

Table 2.11 Alternatives Rescaled According to Discordance Index

Criteria	Car 1	Car 2	Car 3	Car 4
Price	25	50	75	100
MPG	10	20	20	30
Appearance	60	30	60	30
Performance	40	40	20	20

$$d(1, 2) \text{ for price} = (50 - 25)/100 = 0.25$$

$$d(1, 2) \text{ for MPG} = (20 - 10)/100 = 0.1$$

Therefore, $d(1, 2)$ = maximum of $(0.25, 0.1)$ = 0.25. Table 2.12 gives the complete discordance matrix.

Suppose that the decision maker specifies a minimum concordance index of $p = 0.6$ and a maximum discordance index of $q = 0.3$. The following pairs of alternatives satisfy these conditions:

(2, 1)
(3, 1)
(4, 1)
(3, 2)
(4, 2)
(4, 3)

The above relations form the graph shown in Figure 2.14.

Note that Figure 2.14 provides a complete ordering of the alternatives. It shows that: car 4 dominates the remaining cars (that is, it is the most preferred car), car 2 is

Table 2.12 Discordance Matrix for ELECTRE I Example

	Car 1	Car 2	Car 3	Car 4
Car 1	—	0.25	0.5	0.75
Car 2	0.3	—	0.3	0.5
Car 3	0.2	0.2	—	0.25
Car 4	0.3	0.2	0.3	—

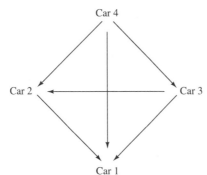

Figure 2.14 Preference Ordering of Alternatives

dominated by cars 3 and 4, and car 1 is dominated by the remaining cars (it is the least preferred car). This analysis concludes that car 4 is the best alternative.

Note, too, that the above analysis can be repeated for different values of p and q to see the impact on the ranking of alternatives. For example, if the decision maker specifies a minimum concordance index of $p = 0.75$ and a maximum discordance index of $q = 0.2$, then the only relations that are satisfied by the concordance and discordance matrices are that car 3 dominates (is preferred to) cars 1 and 2, and that car 4 dominates (is preferred to) car 2. These relationships specify only a partial ordering of the alternatives. They do not, for example, indicate whether car 3 is preferred to car 4, or vice versa. Because of the potential of ELECTRE I to produce a partial ordering of alternatives, other more advanced outranking methods have been developed. One such extension is briefly described below.

2.5.2 ELECTRE II

ELECTRE II is an extension of ELECTRE I that develops a complete ordering of the nondominated solutions. ELECTRE II uses multiple levels of the concordance and discordance conditions (p and q) to construct two extreme outranking conditions. These two relationships are then used to construct two graphs—one depicting strong relationships and the other depicting weak relationships. These two graphs are then used to obtain a complete ranking of the alternatives. For a complete description of this approach see Goicoechea, Hansen, and Duckstein (1982).

2.6 Goal Programming

Goal programming is a multicriteria decision-making approach that facilitates the consideration of multiple conflicting objectives by assigning each a priority. This approach is used when the relationship between the objectives and the decision variables can be expressed mathematically (that is, the approach is used for multiple-objective programming problems).

Goal programming was first proposed by Charnes and Cooper (1961) and Ijiri (1965) for linear models. This method requires the decision maker to specify aspiration levels or goals for each objective. The objective function then specifies the deviations from these goals and the priorities for the achievement of each goal. The idea is to find a feasible point that achieves all the goals "as closely as possible." Because of the conflicting nature of the objectives, a single point that achieves all of the goals probably does not exist.

In order to illustrate goal programming, consider the following multiple-objective programming problem (adapted from Canada and Sullivan, 1989). Suppose a manufacturer produces two types of products, product A and product B. Both products require 1 hour of labor for production. There is a maximum of 10 hours of labor devoted to these two products. The sales quota requires a minimum of 6 units of product A and a minimum of 8 units of product B. The margin of profit is $100.00 for product A and $50.00 for product B. Suppose that the management sets the following goals:

1. Avoid the underutilization of labor.
2. Sell as many of each product as possible, keeping in mind that the profit margin for product A is twice as much as that of product B.
3. Minimize overtime operation.

Let the decision variables of the problem be x_1 and x_2, the number of units of product A and product B to be produced, respectively. The goals stated above can then be expressed as

$$x_1 + x_2 = 10 \qquad \text{(Labor goal)}$$

$$x_1 \geq 6 \qquad \text{(Sales Capacity goal for A)}$$

$$x_2 \geq 8 \qquad \text{(Sales Capacity goal for B)}$$

In order to indicate the deviations from the right-hand side of each goal, negative deviations (d^-) and positive deviations (d^+) are added to the left-hand side of each goal. This results in the following formulation:

$$x_1 + x_2 + d_1^- - d_1^+ = 10$$

$$x_1 + d_2^- - d_2^+ = 6$$

$$x_2 + d_3^- - d_3^+ = 8$$

where d_1^+ is the number of hours over the available 10 hours of labor (overtime operation), d_1^- is the number of unused labor hours (idle time), d_2^- and d_3^- are the shortages of units in meeting the demand for products A and B, respectively, and d_2^+ and d_3^+ are the number of excess units of products A and B produced, respectively.

Assuming that goal 1 is more important than goal 2 and goal 2 is more important than goal 3, priority factors p_1, p_2, and p_3 are assigned to the three goals. Given the deviational factors d_i and the priority factors p_i, the complete goal program can be expressed as

$$\text{Minimize} \quad Z = p_1 d_1^- + 2p_2 d_2^- + p_2 d_3^- + p_3 d_1^+$$

$$\text{subject to} \quad x_1 + x_2 + d_1^- - d_1^+ = 10$$

$$x_1 + d_2^- - d_2^+ = 6 \tag{2-15}$$

$$x_2 + d_3^- - d_3^+ = 8$$

$$x_1, x_2, d_1^+, d_1^-, d_2^+, d_2^-, d_3^+, d_3^- > 0$$

Note that the deviational variables d_2^+ and d_3^+ in Problem (2-15) are not included in the objective function. This is because goal 2 states that the management wants to produce as many of each product as possible and production levels over the stated minimums are permitted. In other words, only underachievements d_2^- and d_3^- are to be minimized. On the other hand, the deviational variables d_1^+ and d_1^- are both included in the objective function because goal 1 demands the use of all available labor hours while goal 3 requires the minimization of labor overtime. Also note that the factor of 2 on d_2^- in the objective function is due to the fact that the profit margin for product A is twice as much as the profit margin for product B.

The above problem has a linear objective function and linear constraints. This problem can be solved using one of several linear programming software packages such as LINDO, GINO, and QSB+. One solution approach to Problem (2-15) is referred to as preemptive goal programming (also called lexicographic GP or non-archimedean GP). In preemptive goal programming the goals are satisfied in an ordinal sequence. These goals are ranked in order of priority by the decision maker and are satisfied sequentially. The highest-priority-level goals are considered to be infinitely more important than the second-priority-level goals, and the second-priority-level goals are considered to be infinitely more important than the third-priority-level goals, and so on. Lower-ranked goals are considered only after the higher-ranked goals are satisfied. The solution to the preemptive goal programming problem is generally obtained by solving a sequence of single-objective problems. The first single-objective problem optimizes with respect to the highest-priority goal. The solution to this goal is then used as a constraint in the optimization with respect to the next-highest-priority goal. The solution to the second problem as well as the first are then used as constraints in the optimization with respect to the third-highest-priority goal, and so on.

Using the preemptive goal programming approach, the optimal solution to Problem (2-15) is $x_1 = 6$, $x_2 = 8$, $d_1^+ = 4$, and $d_1^- = d_2^- = d_3^- = 0$. This solution indicates that 6 units of product 1 and 8 units of product 2 should be produced. This achieves the first two goals completely but cannot satisfy the third goal (because four hours of overtime are needed).

Other popular types of goal programming include archimedean goal programming (also referred to as weighted GP or nonpreemptive GP) and Chebyshev GP (or minimax GP or fuzzy GP). In archimedean goal programming, the objective is to find a solution that minimizes the weighted sum of all unwanted goal deviations. In this case, unlike the preemptive GP, the goals are roughly of the same level of importance. In Chebyshev goal programming, however, one seeks the solution that minimizes the worst unwanted deviation from any single goal. In this case, instead of using subjective notions to set the aspiration levels for the objectives, a set of single optimization problems is solved to arrive at the "best" and the "worst" possible values of each objective. The "best" values are then used as aspiration levels for the objectives. The objective then becomes to minimize the deviation from those aspiration levels so that the worst deviation from any single-goal aspiration level is minimized (Steuer 1986; Ignizio and Cavalier, 1994).

It should be evident from the above discussion that the preference information required from the decision maker in a goal programming problem is much easier to obtain than that required in the assessment of MAUT and MAV functions. It is usually easier for the decision maker to articulate aspiration levels and priorities than to express utility and trade-off weights. Note that GP is applicable only for multiple-objective programming problems where the objectives are expressed mathematically in terms of the decision variables, whereas MAUT and MAV functions may be used for both multiattribute and multiple-objective mathematical programming problems.

Goal programming methods are not without criticisms. One such criticism states that the resulting solution to a goal program may be dominated. That is, there may exist a solution that is better—in terms of some or all of the objectives—than the solution obtained through goal programming. For a discussion of other criticisms of goal programming, see Min and Storbek (1991), which is included in the annotated bibliography of Chapter 5.

2.7 Summary

In this chapter, we have provided the reader with overviews and brief illustrations of several of the more commonly used methods based on the prior articulation of preferences. Recall from Chapter 1 that multiple-criteria decision problems typically fall into two categories: multiattribute problems and multiple-objective programming problems. Numerous techniques have been developed to solve each type of problem. From the descriptions, it is evident that goal programming is a technique that can be used for multiple objective programming problems. Multiattribute value and utility functions can be used for both multiattribute and multiple-objective programming problems. Scoring techniques, the AHP method, and ELECTRE I are used for multiattribute problems. Each of these methods has advantages and disadvantages in terms of the amount and type of information the method requires from the decision maker and the nature of the output it provides (such as ordinal versus cardinal ranking). In Chapter 5, we provide the reader with further discussions of and suggested readings on the suitability of these methods for a given decision problem.

We close this chapter with an annotated bibliography that provides applications of each method. These papers were selected to reflect a broad range of applications in a variety of disciplines. The papers are organized according to the methodology they use.

Annotated Bibliography

Scoring Method

Parsaei, H.R., and M.R. Wilhelm, "A Justification Methodology for Automated Manufacturing Technologies," *Computers and Industrial Eng.,* Vol. 16, No. 3, 1989, pp. 363–373.

Summary: In this paper, scoring methods are used to evaluate and select the appropriate automated manufacturing systems from a list of potential candidates. The authors demonstrate the use of scoring techniques in decision problems where intangible and nonquantifiable elements are present. The proposed methodology uses an additive linear model to rank a firm's long-term and short-term automated manufacturing investment alternatives.

Preference-Based Methods

Brooks, D.G., and C.W. Kirkwood, "Decision Analysis to Select a Microcomputer Networking Strategy: A Procedure and a Case Study," *J. Operational Research Soc.,* Vol. 39, No. 1, 1988, pp. 23–32.

Summary: In this paper, a multiattribute utility function is used to assist a public utility company in selecting an appropriate microcomputer networking strategy. First, the feasible networking strategies are identified. Several evaluation measures, including impact on users, user satisfaction, cost, risk, and compatibility of the system are then defined. Finally, a multiattribute utility function is used to combine these measures into a single index of overall desirability for each networking strategy.

Stanney, K.M., Pet-Edwards, J., Swart, W.W., Safford, R., and T. Barth, "The Design of a Systematic Methods Improvement Planning Methodology: Part II—A Multiattribute Utility Theory (MAUT) Approach," *Int'l J. Industrial Eng.,* Vol. 1, No. 4, 1994, pp. 275–284.

Summary: This proposed methodology uses a multiattribute utility theory (MAUT) approach to prioritize methods improvement techniques that are used for improving productivity at NASA's Kennedy Space Center (KSC). Several improvement criteria, including cycle time, resource utilization, analysis time, and risk are defined in order to rank improvement techniques. The criteria are arranged into a goals tree and their relative importances are assessed. The authors then use an additive value function to determine which methods improvement techniques would be the most cost-effective to implement in order to achieve desired productivity gains.

Analytic Hierarchy Process

Cambron, K.E., and G.W. Evans, "Layout Design Using the Analytic Hierarchy Process," *Computers and Industrial Eng.,* Vol. 20, No. 2, 1991, pp. 211–229.

Summary: Layout design problems are complex problems that require the consideration of multiple conflicting quantitative as well as qualitative criteria. This paper illustrates how the analytic hierarchy process can be used to select the "best" layout design from a set of candidate designs.

Mustafa, M.A., and J. Al-Bahar, "Project Risk Assessment Using the Analytic Hierarchy Process," *IEEE Trans. Eng. Management,* Vol. 38, No. 1, 1991, pp. 46–52.

Summary: This paper describes how the analytic hierarchy process can be used in assessing project risks during the bidding stages. The focus of the paper is specifically on construction projects, and the authors discuss various sources of risks in such projects. The approach is used in assessing the riskiness of constructing the Jamuna Multipurpose Bridge in Bangladesh.

Saaty, T.L., "How to Make a Decision: The Analytic Hierarchy Process," *Interfaces,* Vol. 24, No. 6, 1994, pp. 19–43.

Summary: This paper provides an excellent review of the analytic hierarchy process. Saaty begins by discussing the importance of using a coherent procedure when making a decision. He continues by providing a thorough treatment of the steps involved in any decision-making process. A complete description of the analytic hierarchy process is then given in the context of an application involving the selection of the "best" hospice plan. The problem of rank reversal as well as its resolution is also discussed in this paper.

Outranking Methods

Subramanian, G.H., and M. Gershon, "The Selection of Computer-Aided Software Engineering Tools: A Multi-Criteria Decision Making Approach," *Decision Sciences,* Vol. 22, 1991, pp. 1109–1123.

Summary: The selection of an appropriate computer-aided software engineering (CASE) tool requires the consideration of several criteria, including cost, quality, compatibility, and capability. In this paper, the ELECTRE I method is used to aid the decision maker in generating a preference graph that provides a partial ordering of CASE tools. This paper demonstrates how multiple-criteria decision-making techniques can be applied to software engineering decisions.

Goal Programming

Gupta, J.N.D., and N.U. Ahmed, "A Goal Programming Approach to Job Evaluation," *Computers and Industrial Eng.*, Vol. 14, No. 2, 1988, pp. 147–152.

Summary: This paper illustrates how a linear goal programming approach can be used to systematically evaluate job performance. By considering that each job consists of different levels of various job factors (for example, complexity of duties, education, necessity of supervision, and mental demands), the authors propose using a goal program to evaluate the relative worth of the various levels of factors. This approach is developed in an attempt to make this managerial decision making problem (with multiple objectives) more objective.

References

Bard, J., and S. Sousk, "A Trade-off Analysis for Rough Terrain Cargo Handlers Using the AHP: An Example of Group Decision Making," *IEEE Trans. Eng. Management*, IEEE CS Press, Los Alamitos, Calif., Vol. 37, No. 3, Aug. 1990, pp. 222–228.

Belton, V., "A Comparison of the Analytic Hierarchy Process and a Simple Multiattribute Value Function," *European J. Operational Research*, Vol. 26, 1986, pp. 7–21.

Belton, V., and T. Gear, "On a Shortcoming of Saaty's Method of Analytic Hierarchies," *Omega,* Vol. 11, No. 3, 1983, pp. 228–230.

Boucher, T.O., and E.L. MacStravic, "Multiattribute Evaluation within a Present Value Framework and Its Relation to the Analytic Hierarchy Process," *The Eng. Economist,* Vol. 37, No. 1, Fall 1991, pp. 1–32.

Bunn, D.W., *Applied Decision Analysis,* McGraw-Hill, New York, 1984.

Canada, J.R., and W.G. Sullivan, *Economic and Multiattribute Evaluation of Advanced Manufacturing Systems*, Prentice Hall, Englewood Cliffs, N.J., 1989.

Charnes, A., and W.W. Cooper, *Management Models and Industrial Applications of Linear Programming*, Vol. 1, Wiley, New York, 1961.

Clemen, R.T., *Making Hard Decisions: An Introduction to Decision Analysis,* Duxbury Press, Belmont, Calif., 1991.

Decision Support Software, Inc., *Expert Choice Software Package,* McLean, Va., 1986.

Dyer, J.S., "Remarks on the Analytic Hierarchy Process," *Management Science*, Vol. 36, No. 3, 1990, pp. 249–258.

Edwards, W., "How to Use Multiattribute Utility Measurement for Social Decision Making," *IEEE Trans. Systems, Man, and Cybernetics*, Vol. SMC-7, 1977, pp. 326–340.

Evans, G.W., "An Overview of Techniques for Solving Multiobjective Mathematical Programs," *Management Science*, Vol. 30, No. 11, Nov. 1984, pp. 1268–1282.

French, S., "Interactive Multiobjective Programming: Its Aims, Applications, and Demands," *J. Operational Research Soc.*, Vol. 35, No. 9, 1984, pp. 827–834.

Goicoechea, A., Hansen, D.R., and Duckstein, L., *Multiobjective Decision Analysis with Engineering and Business Applications*, John Wiley and Sons, Inc., New York, 1982.

Golden, B.L., Wasil, E.A., and D.E. Levy, "Applications of the Analytic Hierarchy Process: A Categorized, Annotated Bibliography," in Golden, Wasil, and Harker, *The Analytic Hierarchy Process: Applications and Studies*, Springer-Verlag, Berlin, 1989, pp. 37–58.

Ignizio, J.P., and T.M. Cavalier, *Linear Programming*, Prentice Hall, Englewood Cliffs, N.J., 1994.

Ijiri, Y., *Management Goals and Accounting for Control*, North-Holland Publishing Co., Amsterdam, 1965.

Keeney, R.L., and H. Raiffa, *Decisions with Multiple Objectives: Preferences and Value Trade-offs*, Wiley, New York, 1976.

Kepner, C.H., and B.B. Tregoe, *The New Rational Manager*, Princeton Research Press, Princeton, N.J., 1981.

Min, H. and J. Storbek, "On the Origin and Persistence of Misconceptions in Goal Programming," *J. Operational Research Soc.*, Vol. 42, No. 4, 1991, pp. 301–312.

Mustafa, M., and J. Al-Bahar, "Project Risk Assessment Using the Analytic Hierarchy Process," *IEEE Trans. Eng. Management*, IEEE CS Press, Los Alamitos, Calif., Vol. 38, No. 1, 1991, pp. 46–52.

Saaty, T.L., "A Scaling Method for Priorities in Hierarchical Structures," *J. Math. Psychology*, Vol. 15, 1977, pp. 234–281.

Saaty, T.L., *The Analytic Hierarchy Process*, McGraw-Hill, New York, 1980.

Saaty, T.L., , "Axiomatic Foundation of the Analytic Hierarchy Process," *Management Science*, Vol. 32, No. 7, 1986, pp. 841–855.

Saaty, T.L., "The Analytic Hierarchy Process—What It Is and How It Is Used," *Math. Modeling*, Vol. 9, No. 3–5, 1987, pp. 161–176.

Saaty, T.L., "How to Make a Decision: The Analytic Hierarchy Process," *Interfaces,* Vol. 24, No. 6, 1994, pp. 19–43.

Saaty, T.L., *Decision Making with Dependence and Feedback: The Analytic Network Process*, RWS publications, Pittsburgh, Pa., 1996.

Schoner, B., and W.C. Wedley, "Ambiguous Criteria Weights in AHP: Consequences and Solutions," *Decision Sciences*, Vol. 20, 1989, pp. 462–475.

Steuer, R.E., *Multiple Criteria Optimization: Theory, Computation, and Application*, Wiley, New York, 1986.

Watson, S.R., and A.N.S. Freeling, "Assessing Attribute Weights," *Omega*, Vol. 10, No. 6, 1982, pp. 582–590.

Zahedi, F., "The Analytic Hierarchy Process—A Survey of Methods and Its Applications," *Interfaces*, Vol. 16, 1986, pp. 96–108.

Zeleny, M., *Multiple Criteria Decision Making*, McGraw-Hill, New York, 1982.

Chapter 3

Methods Based on the Progressive Articulation of Preferences

3.1 Introduction

The techniques that rely on progressive articulation of preferences (interactive methods) follow a common pattern. The decision maker is presented with a subset of the nondominated alternatives and is asked to provide some local preference information on these alternatives. This information allows the formulation of a single-criterion subproblem, which is then solved. The new nondominated solution and the outcome are then presented to the decision maker to provide new local information, and the process is repeated until the decision maker either converges toward a best-compromise solution or terminates the process prior to reaching that point. The objective is to find a satisfactory solution after a reasonable number of iterations and within a reasonable amount of time.

Most interactive methods require the generation of a subset of nondominated solutions; the following describes two major approaches for generating such solutions.

3.1.1 Methods Based on Weighting

A common approach to finding nondominated solutions to multiple-objective programming problems is to convert the set of multiple objectives into a single objective through the use of weights. Consider the following multiple-objective programming problem:

$$\text{Minimize} \quad f(x) = [f_1(x), f_2(x), \ldots, f_p(x)]$$

$$\text{subject to} \quad g_j(x) \leq 0 \qquad j = 1, 2, \ldots, m \tag{3-1}$$

where

x is an n-dimensional vector of decision variables,

$f_i(x), i = 1, 2, \ldots, p$ are p distinct objective functions, and

$g_j(x), j = 1, 2, \ldots, m$ are m distinct constraint functions.

The weighting technique transforms Problem (3-1) into the single-objective problem given in (3-2):

$$\text{Minimize} \quad f(x) = [w_1 f_1(x) + w_2 f_2(x) + \ldots + w_p f_p(x)]$$

$$\text{subject to} \quad g_j(x) \leq 0 \qquad j = 1, 2, \ldots, m$$

$$w_1 + w_2 + \ldots + w_p = 1.0 \tag{3-2}$$

$$w_i \geq 0, \qquad i = 1, 2, \ldots, p$$

Given a set of weights that are nonnegative and that sum to one, the solution to Problem (3-2) is a nondominated solution. This means that the approach is guaranteed to generate at least some of the possible nondominated solutions if the weights are varied. If the problem is also convex, then the weighting approach is guaranteed to generate all of the nondominated solutions if all possible weights are explored. Of course, there are an infinite number of possible weights that can be assigned.

3.1.2 Constraint-Based Approaches

Another approach to finding nondominated solutions to multiple-objective programming problems is to convert the set of multiple objectives into a single objective by treating all but one of the objectives as inequality constraints. In this approach, one primary objective $f_k(x)$ is selected to be minimized while the remaining objectives are converted into inequality constraints. Consider the following multiple-objective programming problem:

$$\text{Minimize} \quad f_k(x)$$

$$\text{subject to} \quad g_j(x) \leq 0 \qquad j = 1, 2, \ldots, m \tag{3-3}$$

$$f_i(x) \leq \varepsilon_i, \qquad i = 1, \ldots, p, \ i \neq k$$

If the values of ε_i are chosen so that Problem (3-3) has feasible solutions, then the solution is guaranteed to be nondominated (see Section 5 in Chapter 1 for the definition of a nondominated solution). Therefore, at least some of the nondominated solutions can be discovered by solving Problem (3-3) for specific feasible values of ε_i. In fact, unlike the weighting approach, it turns out that all of the nondominated solutions can be generated if the ε_i's are varied over all possible feasible values—even for problems that are not convex.

3.1.3 Solution Methods

In progressive articulation of preferences, the decision maker may be required to provide one of the following types of information regarding the nondominated solutions or criteria (Evans, Stuckman, and Mollaghasemi, 1991):

1. A ranking of nondominated solutions in the outcome space,
2. A readjustment of aspiration levels from one iteration to the next, or
3. Marginal rates of substitution between the various criteria.

In most cases the required information is less difficult to obtain in an interactive method than in the MAV and MAUT functions.

Methods representative of the interactive methods include the interactive surrogate worth trade-off method (Chankong and Haimes, 1978), the STEP method (Benayoun et al., 1971), Geoffrion-Dyer-Feinberg interactive method (1972), Zionts-Wallenius method (1976), Tchebycheff approach (Steuer and Choo, 1983), and visual interactive goal programming (Korhonen, 1987). Table 3.1 provides a summary of the methods discussed in this chapter. (Note that all of these methods are designed for multiple-objective mathematical programming problems and are not appropriate for multiattribute problems. The output is generally a best-compromise solution.)

Table 3.1   Summary of Interactive Methods

Interactive methods	Method used to generate nondominated solutions	User inputs
Interactive Surrogate Worth Trade-off Method	Constraint-Based Approach	Selection of primary objective and limits on other objectives, worth function
STEP Method	Weighting Method	Trade-off values among objectives
Geoffrion-Dyer-Feinberg	Weighting Method (implicitly defined preference function)	Trade-off values among objectives, selection of best local solution
Zionts and Wallenius	Weighting Method (implicitly defined preference function)	Desirability of trade-offs
Tchebycheff Approach	Weighting Method	Selection of the best local solution
Interactive Visual Goal Programming	Not Applicable	Target values on the goals (aspiration levels) and weights or priorities for deviations from target levels

3.2 Interactive Surrogate Worth Trade-off Method

There are a number of approaches based on examining nondominated solutions generated by either the weighting or the constraint approach. One such approach, the Interactive Surrogate Worth Trade-off Method (ISWT) (Chankong and Haimes, 1978), aids the decision maker in choosing his or her most preferred solution after several solutions have been generated by the constraint approach. The first step is for the decision maker to choose a primary objective and then to provide reasonable values for the right-hand sides of the remaining objectives treated as constraints. The constraint approach is then used to generate a local nondominated solution. Pairwise trade-offs between the primary objective and each of the objectives that have been treated as constraints are determined at the nondominated solution point. The decision maker then provides a worth value (on a scale of -10 to $+10$) for each trade-off. The worth value for each pair of objectives is plotted on a graph to allow the decision maker to change any assessments. If the decision maker is satisfied with the solution, then the algorithm terminates. Otherwise, the worth values are used to generate new values for the right-hand sides of the objectives and the process is repeated.

3.3 STEP Method

The STEP method (STEM) is an interactive method that can be used to identify the best-compromise solution for multiple-objective programming problems. The following is a brief description of the approach. (See Benayoun et al., 1971, for a complete description of this method.)

Assume that, without loss of generality, we wish to maximize p separate linear objective functions, $f_1(x), f_2(x), \ldots, f_p(x)$ of n decision variables, where $x = (x_1, \ldots, x_n)$,

$$f_k(x) = \sum_{j=1}^{n} c_{jk} x_j \tag{3-4}$$

Suppose also that the decision variable values are constrained by $x \in X$, where X is a set of feasible solutions.

The STEP method begins by solving p separate single objective problems as shown in Problem (3-5) (existing software such as LINDO or QSB$^+$ can be used):

$$\text{Maximize} \qquad f_k(x) = \sum_{j=1}^{n} c_{jk} x_j \tag{3-5}$$

$$\text{subject to} \qquad x \in X \qquad \text{for} \quad k = 1, 2, \ldots, p$$

The solution to Problem (3-5), x^k, results in the maximum value of f_k, which is represented by $f_k^M(x^k)$; note that this solution is always a nondominated solution. The values of the remaining objectives at x^k are denoted by f_k^i, for $i = 1, 2, \ldots, p$ and $k \neq i$. By solving the p optimization problems, a $p \times p$ payoff matrix is then constructed.

The diagonal elements of the matrix give an outcome associated with an ideal solution. Unfortunately, because of the conflicting nature of the objectives, an ideal solution usually does not exist. However, the payoff matrix provides the decision maker with a better understanding of the system's multiple-response surface.

The next step involves identifying the nondominated solution with the least deviation from the ideal solution. This is accomplished by solving

$$
\begin{aligned}
\text{Minimize} \quad & d \\
\text{subject to} \quad & \pi_k[f_k^M - f_k(x)] \leq d \qquad k = 1, 2, \ldots, p \\
& x \in X \\
& d \geq 0
\end{aligned}
\tag{3-6}
$$

where

$d = $ maximum deviation of an objective from the ideal solution, and

$\pi_k = $ relative weight of deviation defined as

$$
\pi_k = \frac{\alpha_k}{\displaystyle\sum_{i=1}^{p} \alpha_i}
\tag{3-7}
$$

where

$$
\alpha_k = \left[\frac{f_k^M - f_k^m}{f_k^M} \right] \left[\sum_{j=1}^{n} c_{jk}^2 \right]^{-1/2} \qquad \text{if} \quad f_k > 0,
\tag{3-8}
$$

$$
\alpha_k = \left[\frac{f_k^m - f_k^M}{f_k^m} \right] \left[\sum_{j=1}^{n} c_{jk}^2 \right]^{-1/2} \qquad \text{if} \quad f_k \leq 0.
\tag{3-9}
$$

f_k^M and f_k^m are, respectively, the maximum and the minimum of each column in the payoff matrix (that is, $f_k^m = \text{minimum } [f_k^i, i = 1, \ldots, p]$). It is evident that the values of the weights, π_k, are dependent upon the deviation of the objective from its ideal solution and that the greater this deviation, the larger the magnitude of π_k.

At this point the decision maker is presented with the solution (obtained by solving Problem (3-6)) resulting in the least deviation from the ideal solution. He or she must then identify the satisfactory and unsatisfactory objectives and also indicate which objectives in the current solution can be decreased to achieve an improvement in the unsatisfactory objectives. The constraint set, X, in Problem (3-5) is then modified using this information and the iterations continue until the decision maker is satisfied.

3.4 Geoffrion-Dyer-Feinberg (GDF) Method

The Geoffrion-Dyer-Feinberg (GDF) Interactive Algorithm is a search procedure that moves toward improved feasible solutions through interactions with the decision maker at each step. In this method, the explicit knowledge of the decision maker's overall preferences is not necessary. Throughout the questioning sessions, the decision maker provides local information regarding his preferences which is used to determine the direction toward improved solutions. Once such a direction is established, the decision maker is again solicited to provide information for determining what the step length in this direction should be. The search is terminated when the decision maker is satisfied with a solution or when the improvement between two steps is less than some specified value.

The GDF algorithm is based on the well-known Frank-Wolfe algorithm (1956). This particular algorithm was selected due to its simplicity, convenience, and theoretical properties. (For a detailed description of the Frank-Wolfe algorithms see Geoffrion, Dyer, and Feinberg, 1972).

Consider the following multiple-objective programming problem:

$$\text{Maximize} \quad U(f_1(\boldsymbol{x}), \ldots, f_p(\boldsymbol{x}))$$
$$\text{subject to} \quad \boldsymbol{x} \in X \tag{3-10}$$

where $f_1, \ldots, f_p$ are p functionally independent criterion functions and U is the decision maker's overall preference function defined over the objective space. The functions f_i are assumed to be concave and continuously differentiable on $\boldsymbol{x}$, and the preference function U is assumed to be concave increasing and continuously differentiable on the objective space. The functions f_i and the set X are assumed to be given, while the preference function U is not assumed to be explicitly known.

In order to solve the direction-finding problem using the Frank-Wolfe algorithm the following problem must be solved:

$$\text{Maximize} \quad \nabla_x U[f_1(\boldsymbol{x}^k), \ldots, f_p(\boldsymbol{x}^k)] \cdot \boldsymbol{z} \tag{3-11}$$
$$\text{subject to} \quad \boldsymbol{z} \in X$$

where $\boldsymbol{x}^k$ is a feasible solution to problem (3-10). The solution to Problem (3-11), $\boldsymbol{z}^k$, leads to the determination of the optimal direction, $\boldsymbol{d}^k$, by letting $\boldsymbol{d}^k = \boldsymbol{z}^k - \boldsymbol{x}^k$, where $\boldsymbol{x}^k$ is an initial feasible solution chosen by the user.

Unfortunately, because the preference function U is not known, the direction-finding problem cannot rely on the gradient of U. Geoffrion et al. (1972) suggest the following approach to solve the direction-finding problem:

$$\text{Maximize} \quad \sum_{i=1}^{p} w_i^k \nabla f_i(\boldsymbol{x}^k) \cdot \boldsymbol{z} \tag{3-12}$$
$$\text{subject to} \quad \boldsymbol{z} \in X$$

where $w_i^k = (\partial U/\partial f_i)^k/(\partial U/\partial f_1)^k$ is the trade-off ratio between f_i criterion and the reference criterion f_1 at the current point $\boldsymbol{x}^k$. Once these trade-offs are obtained from the decision maker, the direction-finding problem (3-12) can be solved. This direction is again obtained by letting $d^k = z^k - x^k$, where x^k is an initial feasible solution chosen by the user and z^k is the solution to Problem (3-12).

The next step is to solve the step-size-determination problem. This can be done by presenting the decision maker with the values of the vector $[f_1(x^k + td^k), \ldots, f_p(x^k + td^k)]$ for various values of t between 0 and 1. Once the decision maker selects a preferred solution, the step-size-determination problem is solved. At this point the decision maker has the option of terminating the search (if the solution is satisfactory) or returning to the direction-finding problem.

The algorithm just described has several significant attributes. First, it is clear that the interaction with the decision maker takes place only in the objective space; this fact is of practical importance because the dimension of the objective space is usually significantly less than the dimension of the decision space. Second, the decision maker becomes increasingly more aware of the nature of the problem and the implications of trade-offs as the algorithm proceeds from iteration to iteration. Third, exact specification of the overall preferences is not required in this algorithm; the only information required is the $p - 1$ trade-offs between objective i ($i = 2, 3, \ldots, p$) and objective 1. Unless a consistency check is desired, consideration of all possible pairwise trade-offs is unnecessary.

3.5 Zionts and Wallenius Method

Zionts and Wallenius (1976) developed a method that interactively uses an implicitly defined utility function. The method uses linear approximations of the objective functions and constraints and assumes that the implicit utility function is a linear function of the original objective functions. Under this approach, the best-compromise solution will be one of the extreme points of the linearized problem. This allows the problem to be solved as a sequence of linear programs using the simplex method (a well-established method for solving single-objective linear programming problems).

To start the method, a linear composite function of the original objectives is constructed using a set of arbitrarily chosen positive weights that sum to one. The resulting single-objective problem is solved using linear programming and a nondominated extreme point is identified. Because this nondominated extreme point may not be the best-compromise solution, adjacent nondominated extreme points are presented to the decision maker for consideration. To accomplish this, each of the adjacent extreme points is tested to see whether it is a nondominated solution (that is, we identify which of the nonbasic variables—those variables that have a value of zero—will result in a nondominated solution if brought into the basis—that is, increased in value). This can be determined by seeing if the introduction of the nonbasic variable will simultaneously improve one objective and degrade others. The trade-offs for each of the nondominated solutions are presented to the decision maker, who decides whether the trade-offs are desirable, undesirable, or neither. Based on this information, the nonbasic variables that would lead to solutions declared by the decision maker to be dominated are identified. A sequence of linear programs is then solved for each of the remaining nonbasic variables that have not been declared dominated. This process leads to a final set of nonbasic variables that will in turn lead to nondominated solutions.

The next step involves interaction with the decision maker. For each of the nonbasic variables that will lead to nondominated solutions, the decision maker is asked whether its associated trade-off vector is desirable, undesirable, or neither. Based on the responses of the decision maker, a set of constraints is constructed from which a new set of weights on the objective functions can be determined. These weights are used to transform the multiple-objective programming problem into a single-objective problem. The resulting single-objective problem is solved using linear programming and a nondominated extreme point is identified. Then the process is repeated.

3.6 Tchebycheff Approach

The Tchebycheff approach was developed by Steuer and Choo (1983). The approach begins with the generation of the ideal point, representing the best value of each objective function. This point is generated by maximizing (or minimizing) each of the objectives separately (as in the STEP method). Next, a large sample of nondominated solutions is generated through the use of the weighting method described earlier and presented to the decision maker, who is thus provided with information on the range of the solutions. This latter set is then filtered through two processes to obtain a reasonable number of nondominated solutions to be presented to the decision maker. The first filtering process creates a subset of the original set by selecting the solutions that are most different in terms of the values of the decision variables. From this subset, the ideal point is used in a second filtering process to select those solutions that are most different in terms of the objective function values. This two-step process ensures that the remaining set includes a manageable number of nondominated solutions and that the solutions represent the entire decision and objective space. The decision maker then selects a most preferred solution from this set. If the solution is satisfactory, the decision maker terminates the search; otherwise, he or she computes ranges for each of the elements in the weighting vector by using the ideal point and the current preferred solution. New nondominated solutions are again generated by randomly selecting weights within the specified ranges. (Note that each iteration reduces the ranges on the weights.) This process continues until the decision maker is satisfied with a solution.

3.7 Interactive and Visual Interactive Goal Programming

Interactive goal programming combines features from both preemptive and archimedean goal programming (described in Chapter 2) in an interactive mode. In this approach the decision maker begins with specifying the type of goal (constraint), which can be in the form of $\leq$, $\geq$, or $=$. The next step involves the specification of the target levels for the goals; these signify the decision maker's aspiration level for each objective. The goals are then grouped into priority levels. That is, the decision maker states which objectives are the most important, the second most important, and so on. Then, within each priority level, the decision maker specifies penalty weights for those priority levels associated with more than one goal. Once set up, the goal program is solved using the preemptive goal programming solution method. At this point the decision maker is presented with the solution and is asked to make any changes in the goal type, aspiration level, priority, or weights that he or she desires. The new problem is then solved and presented to the decision maker for any further adjustments, and the process continues until the decision maker is satisfied with the solution (Steuer, 1986).

Note that in interactive goal programming it is not always clear what the resulting solution will be, because the decision maker may make changes in several factors. That is, this technique is an unstructured and ad hoc approach for exploring the feasible region and may require a great deal of intuition and experience on the part of the decision maker. In spite of that, interactive goal programming is widely used because of its simplicity and the availability of linear programming software packages such as LINDO, QSB⁺.

Visual interactive goal programming (VIG), developed by Korhonen (1987), is a visual search procedure that is an extension of interactive goal programming. One enhancement of VIG is that the user can visually observe the effect of changing the aspiration levels at each stage. VIG allows the user to search the efficient (Pareto-optimal) frontier of a multiple-objective linear programming problem. By searching the efficient frontier, the system only presents the decision maker with efficient, nondominated solutions and inferior solutions are eliminated automatically (Kananen, Korhonen, Wallenius, and Wallenius, 1990).

The system presents the values of the objectives numerically and as bar graphs on the computer screen. By allowing the user to control the direction and speed of the motion, the length of the bars change on the screen dynamically as the decision maker travels on the efficient frontier. In effect, this allows the user to change the right-hand side of the equations simultaneously and to visualize how improving one or more objectives would affect other objectives. (VIG is a user-friendly software package that is written in TURBO PASCAL. For mathematical details of VIG, see Korhonen and Laakso, 1986, or Steuer, 1986.)

Annotated Bibliography

Surrogate Worth Trade-off Method

Sakawa, M., "Multiobjective Optimization for a Standby System by the Surrogate Worth Trade-off Method," *J. Operational Research Society*, Vol. 31, 1980, pp. 153–158.

Summary: This paper discusses the application of the Surrogate Worth Trade-off Method (SWT) to the problem of standby redundancy systems. The author formulates a multiobjective mathematical model of the system in order to optimize system reliability, cost, weight, and volume under constraints. SWT method is used to resolve conflicts between the objectives.

STEP Method (STEM)

Loucks, D.P., "An Application of Interactive Multiobjective Water Resources Planning," *Interfaces*, Vol. 8, No. 1, 1977, pp. 70–75.

Summary: Loucks describes how the STEP Method is used in a water resources planning project in North Africa. The objective of the project is to aid government officials in choosing the best compromise among three conflicting objectives: maximize water yield, maximize yield reliability, and minimize total cost. The solution yields a single plan for each irrigation area.

Geoffrion-Dyer-Feinberg Method (GDF)

Geoffrion, A.M., Dyer, J.S., and A. Feinberg, "An Interactive Approach for Multicriterion Optimization, with an Application to the Operation of an Academic Department," *Management Science*, Vol. 19, No. 4, 1972, pp. 357–368.

Summary: The authors provide a detailed description of the GDF method as well as the Frank-Wolf algorithm. In addition, an application of the GDF algorithm to the operation of an academic department is described. This approach is used to assist in planning the future operations of the department in terms of course offerings at the graduate and undergraduate levels, amount of teaching-assistant time used for classroom support, and amount of faculty time devoted to research and service.

Zionts and Wallenius Method

Korhonen, P., and M. Soismaa, "An Interactive Multiple Criteria Approach to Ranking Alternatives," *J. Operational Research Society*, Vol. 32, 1981, pp. 577–585.

Summary: Here the Zionts and Wallenius Method is applied to ranking 15 countries according to their economic performance. The six criteria used in ranking the alternatives are: the percentage change in the gross national product (GNP) from the previous year, reported unemployment, inflation, trade deficit, labor cost per production unit, and industrial investments.

Weighted Tchebycheff Method

Stam, A., and L. Gardiner, "A Multiple Objective Marketing-Manufacturing Approach for Order (Market) Selection," *Computers and Operation Research,* Vol. 19, No. 7, 1992, pp. 571–583.

Summary: This paper discusses the need for interfunctional coordination between marketing and manufacturing departments when deciding which orders to accept. The authors propose a three-phase approach to enhance interfunctional integration. Model formulation is the first phase, during which the functional and corporate objectives, goals, and constraints are identified and modeled. After Phase 1 the approach iterates between Phase 2 and Phase 3. In Phase 2 the Tchebycheff Method is employed to generate a set of nondominated solutions (order portfolios) for consideration by the decision maker(s). Then in Phase 3 the decision maker(s) evaluate the alternatives and select the most preferred order portfolio. The evaluation in this phase may lead to the modification of the model and the start of the next iteration. This iterative process terminates when the marketing and manufacturing decision makers reach consensus. The approach is illustrated using an example from a small manufacturing company that produces custom items.

Visual Interactive Goal Programming (VIG)

Kananen, I., Korhonen, P., Wallenius, J., and H. Wallenius, "Multiple Objective Analysis of Input-Output Mode for Emergency Management," *Operations Research*, Vol. 38, No. 2, 1990, pp. 193–201.

Summary: This paper describes an application of the Visual Interactive Goal (VIG) Programming. The approach is applied to analyzing the quantitative impacts of economic and political crisis to the Finnish economy. The effects of several emergency management situations, including energy crisis, nuclear power plant accidents, trade embargo, and labor shortage are discussed.

Stam, A., and M. Kuula, "Selecting a Flexible Manufacturing System Using Multiple Criteria Analysis," *Int'l J. Production Research*, Vol. 29, No. 4, 1991, pp. 803–820.

Summary: This paper describes a visual interactive decision support system that can aid top management in selecting the most appropriate flexible manufacturing system (FMS) design. The proposed approach consists of two phases. In the initial phase, the analytic hierarchy process is used to narrow down the large list of candidate FMS configurations to a manageable number (typically three or four most attractive alternatives). The second phase involves using Korhonens VIG package to solve a multiobjective mathematical program in which the alternatives are explored interactively. In this phase the decision maker evaluates the trade-offs between various decision criteria such as production volume, cost, and flexibility to arrive at the best solution. The application of this approach to a Finnish metal product firm is described.

References

Benayoun, R., de Montgolfier, J., Tergny, J., and O. Laritchev, "Linear Programming and Multiple Objective Functions: STEP Method (STEM)," *Math. Programming*, Vol. 1, No. 3, 1971, pp. 366–375.

Chankong, V., and Y.Y. Haimes, "The Interactive Surrogate Worth Trade-Off (ISWT) Method for Multiobjective Decision-Making," in *Vol. of Multi-Criteria Problem Solving*, S. Zionts (ed.), Springer-Verlag, New York, 1978.

Evans, G.W., Stuckman, B., and M. Mollaghasemi, "Multiple Response Simulation Optimization," *Proc. 1991 Winter Simulation Conf.*, 1991, pp. 894–900.

Frank, M., and P. Wolfe, "An Algorithm for Quadratic Programming," *Econometrica*, Vol. 24, 1956, pp. 253–263.

Geoffrion, A.M., Dyer, J.S., and A. Feinberg, "An Interactive Approach for Multicriterion Optimization, with an Application to the Operation of an Academic Department," *Management Science*, Vol. 19, No. 4, 1972, pp. 357–368.

Kananen, I., Korhonen, P., Wallenius, J., and H. Wallenius, "Multiple Objective Analysis of Input-Output Mode for Emergency Management," *Operations Research*, Vol. 38, No. 2, 1990, pp. 193–201.

Korhonen, P., "VIG—A Visual Interactive Support System for Multiple Criteria Decision Making," *Belgian J. Operations Research, Statistics, and Computer Science*, Vol. 27, 1987, pp. 3–15.

Korhonen, P., and J. Laakso, "A Visual Interactive Method for Solving the Multiple Criteria Problem," *European J. Operational Research*, Vol. 24, 1986, pp. 277–287.

Steuer, R.E., *Multiple Criteria Optimization: Theory, Computation and Application*, Wiley, New York, 1986.

Steuer, R.E., and E.-U. Choo, "An Interactive Weighted Tchebycheff Procedure for Multiple Objective Programming," *Math. Programming*, Vol. 26, No. 1, 1983, pp. 326–344.

Zionts, S., and J. Wallenius, "An Interactive Programming Method for Solving the Multiple Criteria Problem," *Management Science*, Vol. 22, No. 6, 1976, pp. 652–663.

Chapter 4

Methods Based on the Posterior Articulation of Preferences

4.1 Introduction

The techniques that rely on posterior articulation of preferences are the least commonly used of the multicriteria approaches. The majority of the methods in this category are applied to multiple-objective mathematical programming problems. These methods try first to find all or almost all of the nondominated solutions to the problem. The nondominated solutions are then presented to the decision maker to select the preferred one through elicitation of preference information. Because multiple-objective problems usually have an infinite number of nondominated solutions, choosing a single preferred solution can be very cumbersome. Note, however, that there are techniques available for reducing a large set of nondominated solutions to a manageable number (see, for example, Graves et al., 1992).

Many of the posterior approaches have been modified into interactive (progressive) methods. For example, the surrogate worth trade-off method (Haimes and Hall, 1974) was originally designed as a posterior method, where the set of nondominated solutions were generated using the constraint approach, preference information (based on the trade-offs among the objectives) was obtained from the decision maker to establish his or her worth function, and then a single-objective mathematical programming problem was constructed to find the decision makers preferred solution. This method was subsequently modified into the interactive surrogate worth trade-off method (see Chapter 3 and Chankong and Haimes, 1978).

As with the interactive methods, posterior methods generally require the generation of nondominated solutions through either the weighting or the constraint approach. The decision maker is then required to provide one of several types of information regarding the nondominated solutions (for example, preferences among the nondominated solutions or preferences for trade-offs between the objectives). In most cases, the information required in a posterior method is more cumbersome to obtain than in the progressive methods because of the size of the set of nondominated solutions; however, the information is elicited only once.

Because the posterior methods are similar (in terms of the level of complexity) to the methods described in Chapter 3, and very few of them are used today, we have elected to describe only one: the data envelopment method (DEA). Although DEA does not explicitly use preference information from the decision maker, we have classified it as a posterior method because it is used to analyze the efficiency of sets of alternatives. After applying DEA, the decision maker will often use the information generated by the method in making more informed choices about the alternatives. Since DEA is a widely used approach in a variety of applications (see Seiford, 1990), we feel this posterior method may prove useful to the reader.

4.2 Data Envelopment Analysis (DEA)

Data envelopment analysis was originated by Charnes, Cooper, and Rhodes (1978) as a methodology to analyze the relative efficiency of each of several decision making units (DMUs). DMUs may be thought of as alternatives in the context of a multiple-criteria problem, although that is not the usual application context. DEA has proven to be a popular method for analyzing a wide variety of operations and systems, including hospitals, pharmacies, restaurants, schools, colleges, Air Force tactical fighter wings, agricultural systems, mining operations, program evaluation, computer system designs, electric utilities, site selection, software development, and manufacturing (see Seiford, 1990, for a list of nearly 400 articles, reports, and theses related to DEA). As described and illustrated in the following sections, DEA takes a fundamentally different viewpoint from the other multiple-criteria approaches described in this book, because it explicitly considers inputs and outputs that are associated with each of the alternatives (or DMUs).

4.2.1 The Basic Elements of DEA

The basic elements of a DEA analysis are the decision making units (DMUs), inputs (where less is better), and outputs (where more is better). A decision making unit is any entity for which measurable inputs and outputs can be assigned. For example, DMUs may be schools, hospitals, manufacturing processes, or city governments. The inputs may be the number of employees, the advertising expenses, and various types of assets used in production. The outputs may be profits, performance indicators (such as throughput), or quality measures. The viewpoint taken is that an increase in an input is expected to yield an increase in an output. For example, increasing the advertising of a product is expected to result in increased sales. However, the viewpoint is also that it is desirable to minimize inputs because the inputs require resources and thus result in a cost. In the context of a multicriteria problem, the DMUs can be considered to be the alternatives and the outputs can be considered to be the criteria. It should also be noted that the inputs could be viewed as attributes that we would like to minimize.

DEA analysis provides several useful results. It constructs the so-called envelopment surface (also called a production function or efficient frontier). This allows one to determine which of the DMUs (alternatives) are efficient and which are inefficient. Note that the concept of efficiency can be related to Pareto optimality when the envelopment surface is derived using a linear model. The envelopment surface shows the maximum amount of outputs that can be achieved by combining various inputs. Alternatively, it shows the minimum amount of inputs required to achieve a given output level.

DEA analysis also establishes an inefficiency metric. The envelopment surface is considered to be the best practice associated with the most efficient operations. The inefficiency metric allows one to evaluate other DMUs (alternatives) based on their distance to the envelopment surface (frontier). DEA analysis can identify the sources and degrees of the inefficiencies. It can also provide a projection mapping that tells us how to move from an inefficient DMU to the efficient frontier (that is, the envelopment surface). Finally, DEA analysis also provides the decision maker with an efficient reference set. In other words, it provides a list of DMUs (alternatives) that are considered to be efficient and can be used as a benchmark for comparison.

There is a distinct difference between methods based on central tendency (for example, regression) and DEA. Instead of fitting a hyperplane through the center of the data, a piecewise linear surface is generated on top of the observations. Graphically, one could view the difference between the two approaches as shown in Figure 4.1,

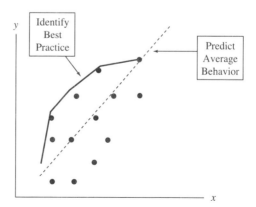

Figure 4.1   Illustration of the Distinction Between DEA and Methods Based on Central Tendency

where the x coordinate represents the input values (independent variables) and the y coordinate represents the output values (dependent variables). DEA focuses on the individual DMUs (alternatives or observations) rather than averaging the observations.

As noted by Seiford (1994), the additive (BCC) model (Charnes et al., 1985) relates efficiency results to the concept of Pareto optimality. The CCR ratio model (Charnes et al., 1978) provides a distinction between technical versus scale inefficiencies. The multiplicative models (Charnes et al., 1982, 1983) provide a log-linear or a Cobb-Douglas interpretation of the production process (envelopment frontier). We have chosen to present only the basics for the additive model, because it is most closely related to generating and evaluating Pareto optimal solutions. (See the above citations for additional information about other DEA models.)

4.2.2 The DEA Linear Programming Formulation

The approach used to develop the envelopment frontier is based on the additive model, and it uses a pair of dual linear programming models as shown below. In particular, the following formulation is used: given m inputs, p outputs, and n DMUs, let x_{ij} correspond to the value of the ith input variable $(i = 1, 2, \ldots, m)$ for the jth DMU $(j = 1, 2, \ldots, n)$, and let y_{kj} correspond to the value of the kth output variable $(k = 1, 2, \ldots, p)$ for the jth DMU.

Primal Problem for the jth DMU:

$$\text{Minimize} \quad -\sum_{i=1}^{p} s_i - \sum_{i=1}^{m} \varepsilon_i$$

$$\text{subject to} \quad \sum_{l=1}^{n} \lambda_l y_{il} - s_i = y_{ij} \qquad i = 1, 2, \ldots, p$$

$$-\sum_{l=1}^{n} \lambda_l x_{il} - \varepsilon_i = -x_{ij} \qquad i = 1, 2, \ldots, m$$

$$\sum_{i=1}^{n} \lambda_i = 1$$

$$\lambda_i, \varepsilon_i, s_i \geq 0 \quad \text{for all } i$$

Dual Problem for the jth DMU:

$$\text{Maximize} \quad \sum_{i=1}^{p} \mu_i y_{ij} - \sum_{i=1}^{m} \nu_i x_{ij} + \omega_j$$

$$\text{subject to} \quad \sum_{i=1}^{p} \mu_i y_{ik} - \sum_{i=1}^{m} \nu_i x_{ik} + \omega_j \leq 0 \qquad k = 1, 2, \ldots, n$$

$$-\mu_i \leq -1 \qquad i = 1, 2, \ldots, p$$

$$-\nu_i \leq -1 \qquad i = 1, 2, \ldots, m$$

$$\omega_j \quad free$$

Note that only one of the preceding problems needs to be solved for the jth DMU. The results for the other problem can be obtained through sensitivity analysis. The reader is referred to any operations research text to understand the relationship between the primal and the dual problems (see, for example, Winston, 1995).

An underlying concept of DEA is the notion of efficiency. In the dual problem, the variables correspond to prices for the inputs and outputs. Efficiency is defined to be the sum of the value of the outputs divided by the sum of the value of the inputs. It is assumed that no DMU (or alternative) can be more than 100 percent efficient. Consequently, we obtain constraints of the form:

$$\frac{\sum\limits_{i=1}^{p} \mu_i y_{ik}}{\sum\limits_{i=1}^{m} \nu_i x_{ik}} \leq 1.0 \quad k = 1, 2, \ldots n$$

By multiplying both sides of the inequality by the denominator, we obtain linear expressions that become part of the dual problem.

The primal problem is called the envelopment form, while the dual problem is called the multiplier form. The primal and dual problems are solved for each of the n DMUs. When the optimal objective functions (for both the primal and the dual) are equal to zero, then the jth DMU is on the efficient frontier. If the DMU is not efficient, then some of the s_i and/or ε_i elements are not equal to zero, and these nonzero elements identify both the sources and the amounts of inefficiency in the corresponding inputs and outputs. In the dual problem, the value of the objective function for inefficient DMUs provides a measure of the distance of the DMU to the closest supporting hyperplane (on the efficient frontier). The values of the dual variables for efficient DMUs provide an economic interpretation as the rates of substitution of the inputs for the outputs along the efficient frontier.

4.2.3 An Illustration of DEA

The following example of DEA was adapted from Winston (1995). To understand how DEA works, consider three hospitals (DMUs). Suppose that each hospital uses two inputs to produce three outputs. Namely, the inputs are capital (measured by the number of hospital beds) and labor (measured by labor hours per month); the outputs are hundreds of patient-days during the month for (a) patients under age 14, (b) patients

Table 4.1   Input and Output Data for
Three Alternative Hospitals

Hospital	Inputs		Output		
	1	2	1	2	3
1	5	14	9	4	16
2	8	15	5	7	10
3	7	12	4	9	13

between 14 and 65, and (c) patients over 65. The inputs and outputs for the three hospitals are summarized in Table 4.1.

Using the preceding LP formulation for the dual problem, the following LPs are solved:

Dual Problem for Hospital 1:

$$\text{Maximize} \quad 9\mu_1 + 4\mu_2 + 16\mu_3 - 5\nu_1 - 14\nu_2 + \omega_1$$

$$\text{subject to} \quad 9\mu_1 + 4\mu_2 + 16\mu_3 - 5\nu_1 - 14\nu_2 + \omega_1 \leq 0$$

$$5\mu_1 + 7\mu_2 + 10\mu_3 - 8\nu_1 - 15\nu_2 + \omega_1 \leq 0$$

$$4\mu_1 + 9\mu_2 + 13\mu_3 - 7\nu_1 - 12\nu_2 + \omega_1 \leq 0$$

$$\mu_i \geq 1 \quad i = 1, 2, 3$$

$$\nu_i \geq 1 \quad i = 1, 2$$

Dual Problem for Hospital 2:

$$\text{Maximize} \quad 5\mu_1 + 7\mu_2 + 10\mu_3 - 8\nu_1 - 15\nu_2 + \omega_2$$

$$\text{subject to} \quad 9\mu_1 + 4\mu_2 + 16\mu_3 - 5\nu_1 - 14\nu_2 + \omega_2 \leq 0$$

$$5\mu_1 + 7\mu_2 + 10\mu_3 - 8\nu_1 - 15\nu_2 + \omega_2 \leq 0$$

$$4\mu_1 + 9\mu_2 + 13\mu_3 - 7\nu_1 - 12\nu_2 + \omega_2 \leq 0$$

$$\mu_i \geq 1 \quad i = 1, 2, 3$$

$$\nu_i \geq 1 \quad i = 1, 2$$

Dual Problem for Hospital 3:

$$\text{Maximize} \quad 4\mu_1 + 9\mu_2 + 13\mu_3 - 7\nu_1 - 12\nu_2 + \omega_3$$

$$\text{subject to} \quad 9\mu_1 + 4\mu_2 + 16\mu_3 - 5\nu_1 - 14\nu_2 + \omega_3 \leq 0$$

Table 4.2 Objective Function Values for the
Three Hospitals

	Original value of the objective	**Final value of the objective**
Hospital 1	0	0
Hospital 2	0	–6.6
Hospital 3	0	0

$$5\mu_1 + 7\mu_2 + 10\mu_3 - 8\nu_1 - 15\nu_2 + \omega_3 \leq 0$$
$$4\mu_1 + 9\mu_2 + 13\mu_3 - 7\nu_1 - 12\nu_2 + \omega_3 \leq 0$$
$$\mu_i \geq 1 \qquad i = 1, 2, 3$$
$$\nu_i \geq 1 \qquad i = 1, 2$$

The "Problem Solver" in Microsoft EXCEL was used to solve the preceding problems. For illustration purposes, selected output is shown below. Specifically, the objective function values for all hospitals, the optimal solution values for hospital 3, and the sensitivity analysis for hospital 2 are shown in Tables 4.2, 4.3, and 4.4, respectively.

As shown in Table 4.2, the values of the objective function at the optimal solution for hospitals 1, 2, and 3 are 0, –6.6, and 0, respectively. Thus we see that hospitals 1

Table 4.3 Optimal Solution Values for
Hospital 3

Variable	**Original value**	**Final value**
μ_1	0	2.4
μ_2	0	1
μ_3	0	1
ν_1	0	1
ν_2	0	1
ω_1	0	0
ω_2	0	0
ω_3	0	–12.6

Table 4.4 Sensitivity Analysis for Hospital 2

Constraint	Final value	Shadow price	Constraint R.H. side	Allowable increase	Allowable decrease
Output 1	−1.77636E-15	0.2	0	33	7
Output 2	−6.6	0	0	1E + 30	6.6
Output 3	1.77636E-15	0.8	0	7	1E + 30
Input 1	2.4	0	1	1.4	1E + 30
Input 2	1	−1	1	1E + 30	1.4

and 3 are efficient (lie on the efficient frontier) and hospital 2 is inefficient (that is, hospital 2 is dominated by hospitals 1 and 3). The value of −6.6 is a measure of the distance of hospital 2 from the efficient frontier.

The results for hospital 3, shown in Table 4.3, indicate that the rate of substitution (economic value) of output 1 (that is, μ_1) is 2.4 times that of any other inputs or outputs. Thus, output 1 has a much greater impact than any of the other inputs or outputs.

From the sensitivity analysis in Table 4.4 we see that the shadow prices for hospital 2, which correspond to the values of the slacks in the primal problem for the inefficient hospital (the reader is again referred to Winston, 1995 for further elaboration), indicate that outputs 1 and 3, and input 2 are the sources of the inefficiencies. Their corresponding values, 0.2, 0.8, and −1 indicate the amount of the inefficiency.

4.3 Concluding Remarks

As discussed earlier, posterior methods place a great deal of cognitive burden on the decision maker and hence are the least popular of the MCDM classes of methods. Although DEA is not explicitly classified as a posterior method in the literature, we have classified it as a posterior method because it is used to analyze the efficiency of sets of alternatives. Since DEA is a widely used approach in a variety of applications (see Seiford 1990), we feel that this posterior method may prove useful to the reader.

Annotated Bibliography

Charnes, A., Cooper, W.W., Golany, B., and L.M. Seiford, "Foundations of Data Envelopment Analysis for Pareto-Koopmans Efficient Empirical Production Functions," *J. Econometrics*, Vol. 30, No. 1/2, 1985, pp. 91–107.

Summary: This paper describes the linear additive model. This is one of the simpler DEA models and is equivalent to identifying and analyzing Pareto optimal solutions.

Charnes, A., Cooper, W.W., and E. Rhodes, "Measuring the Efficiency of Decision Making Units," *European J. Operational Research*, Vol. 2, No. 6, 1978, pp. 429–444.

Summary: This paper describes the original development of DEA. It also discusses technical versus scale inefficiencies.

Charnes, A., Cooper, W.W., Seiford, L.M., and J. Stutz, "A Multiplicative Model for Efficiency Analysis," *Socio-Economic Planning Sciences*, Vol. 16, No. 5, 1982, pp. 223–224.

Summary: This paper describes and illustrates a multiplicative model for DEA.

Charnes, A., Cooper, W.W., Seiford, L.M., and J. Stutz, "Invariant Multiplicative Efficiency and Piecewise Cobb-Douglas Envelopments," *Operations Research Letters*, Vol. 2, No. 3, 1983, pp. 101–103.

Summary: This paper describes and illustrates a multiplicative model for DEA.

Seiford, L.M., "A Bibliography of Data Envelopment Analysis (1978–1990), Version 5," tech. report, Dept. Industrial Eng. and Operations Research, Univ. of Massachusetts, Amherst, Mass., 1990.

Summary: This report contains a bibliography of over 400 articles, reports, and dissertations related to DEA. It covers the years 1978–1990.

Seiford, L.M., "Data Envelopment Analysis: Learning from Outliers," 1st Industrial Eng. Research Conf. Proc., 1992, pp. 437–441.

Summary: This paper provides a brief overview of DEA. It illustrates one of the DEA models and discusses some extensions.

References

Chankong, V. and Y.Y. Haimes, *The Interactive Surrogate Worth Trade-off (ISWT) Method for Multiobjective Decision Making*, 1978, Springer, New York.

Charnes, A., Cooper, W.W., Golany, B., and L.M. Seiford, "Foundations of Data Envelopment Analysis for Pareto-Koopmans Efficient Empirical Production Functions," *J. Econometrics*, Vol. 30, No. 1/2, 1985, pp. 91–107.

Charnes, A., Cooper, W.W., and E. Rhodes, "Measuring the Efficiency of Decision Making Units," *European J. Operational Research*, Vol. 2, No. 6, 1978, pp. 429–444.

Charnes, A., Cooper, W.W., Seiford, L.M., and J. Stutz, "A Multiplicative Model for Efficiency Analysis," *Socio-Economic Planning Sciences*, Vol. 16, No. 5, 1982, pp. 223–224.

Charnes, A., Cooper, W.W., Seiford, L.M., and J. Stutz, "Invariant Multiplicative Efficiency and Piecewise Cobb-Douglas Envelopments," *Operations Research Letters*, Vol. 2, No. 3, 1983, pp. 101–103.

Graves, S.B., Ringuest, J.L., and J. Bard, "Recent Developments in Screening Methods for Non-dominated Solutions in Multiobjective Optimization," *Computers and Operations Research*, Vol. 19, No. 7, 1992, pp. 683–694.

Haimes, Y.Y. and W.A. Hall, "Multiobjectives in Water Resources Systems Analysis: The Surrogate Worth Trade-off Method," *Water Resources Research*, Vol. 10, 1974, pp. 14–624.

Seiford, L.M., "A Bibliography of Data Envelopment Analysis (1978–1990), Version 5," tech. report, Dept. Industrial Eng. and Operations Research, Univ. of Massachusetts, Amherst, Mass., 1990.

Seiford, L.M., "Data Envelopment Analysis: What, Why and How, a Tutorial," TIMS/ORSA Conf. Presentation, Boston, Mass., Apr. 26, 1994.

Winston, W.L., *Introduction to Mathematical Programming*, Duxbury Press, Belmont, Calif., 1995.

A Guide to Readers

5.1. Overview of Methods

We have presented several different methods for solving multiple-criteria decision problems. We briefly described and illustrated each method and provided reference to at least one application from the literature in the annotated bibliographies. The information presented in Chapters 1 through 4 should provide the reader with some ideas on how each method works and the types of applications where each may be used. We noted earlier that multiple-criteria methods differ by the type of problem they are designed to solve (that is, multiattribute versus multiobjective), the timing of the decision makers information (for example, prior versus progressive), the type of information required from the decision maker (for example, pairwise comparisons of alternatives, lotteries, trade-offs, values, and so on), and the availability of supporting software. Table 5.1 summarizes the information about each method described in this book. The reader can examine this table to determine whether one or more of the methods might be appropriate for use in a particular decision-making situation. In the remainder of this chapter, we discuss the advantages and the disadvantages of each method, provide a guide for selecting an appropriate method, and, finally, reference several papers that can further guide the reader in choosing from among the various multiple-criteria methods.

Table 5.1 Taxonomy of Multiple-Criteria Decision-Making Techniques

MCDM methods	Type of problem			Nature of DM information			Type of DM information required	Commercially available software
	*Multi-objective	†Multi-attribute	‡Uncertainty	Prior	Progressive	Posterior		
Scoring Method		✓		✓			Scores on attributes and objectives	None (method is simple enough to develop on a spreadsheet)
Multiattribute Value Function	✓	✓		✓			Weights and value functions on attributes	SMART, HIPRE 3+, Criterium, Decision-Plus, CPME, VISA II
Multiattribute Utility Function	✓	✓	✓	✓			Weights and utility functions on attributes using lotteries	Continuous Multi-attribute Risk, CPME, Logical Decisions for Windows
Analytic Hierarchy Process		✓		✓			Pairwise comparisons of attributes and alternatives	Expert Choice, Criterium Decision-Plus, Criterium DOS v.1.1, HIPRE 3+
ELECTRE I, II, III		✓		✓			Rating scale for criteria weights and discordance index	None (method is simple enough to develop on a spreadsheet)
Goal Programming	✓	✓		✓			Priorities and aspiration levels on goals	QSB+, any LP problem solver can be used
Data Envelopment Analysis		✓				✓§	No DM preferences are used	None, but any LP or NLP problem solver can be used
Interactive Surrogate Worth Trade-off Method	✓				✓		Limits on objectives and worth values on trade-offs	None, but any LP or NLP problem solver can be used to solve subproblems

Method					
STEP	✓		Degree of satisfaction of objectives	✓	None, but any LP or NLP problem solver can be used to solve subproblems
GDF	✓		Trade-off between objectives and solution preferences	✓	None, but any LP or NLP problem solver can be used to solve subproblems
Zionts and Wallenius	✓		Desirability of trade-offs	✓	None, but any LP or NLP problem solver can be used to solve subproblems
Tchebycheff	✓		Selection of most preferred solution and ranges of weights on the objectives	✓	None, but any LP or NLP problem solver can be used to solve subproblems
Interactive Goal Programming	✓		Priorities on goals, penalty weights	✓	None, but any LP or NLP problem solver can be used to solve subproblems

*Explicit mathematical relationships between the decision variables and the objectives and constraints must be constructed. The criteria are generally based on objective measures such as cost, profit, and resource requirements.

†Decision problems where both objective and subjective (for example, prestige, comfort, flexibility) criteria are involved. No mathematical relationship must be defined between the alternatives and the objectives.

‡MAUT is the only method that was designed to handle decision problems with uncertain outcomes. Note that the impact of uncertainty may be analyzed in other methods through the use of sensitivity analysis.

§DEA analyzes the efficiency of a set of alternatives. It does not determine the most preferred solution and does not require preference input from the decision maker.

5.2 Advantages and Disadvantages of MCDM Methods

In this section we summarize the techniques presented in Chapters 2 through 4. We then provide a discussion of each technique's advantages and disadvantages.

5.2.1 Methods Based on the Prior Articulation of Preferences

Methods grouped within this general approach solve multiple-criteria decision problems by first determining the decision makers preference structure. Once the decision makers preferences are obtained, the problem can be solved using some type of analytical strategy. The advantages of this approach can be summarized as follows: (1) the process of determining a preference structure helps the decision maker to explore and understand the problem better, and (2) once the decision maker's preference structure is articulated, analytical methods can be used to solve the problem. The primary disadvantage of this class of methods is that the process of determining the preference structure is often difficult and time-consuming.

I. **Scoring methods.**   Scoring methods are among the simplest and, probably, most popular tools for solving multiattribute decision problems. Given n alternatives and m attributes, the decision maker first assigns weights, w_i ($i = 1, \ldots, m$), to each of the m attributes. In order to assess these weights, the relative importance of each attribute is determined by the decision maker on a scale of 1 to 10 or 1 to 100. The next step requires the decision maker to evaluate how well each of the n alternatives performs with respect to each of the m attributes. In order to accomplish this, a numerical value, a_{ij} ($i = 1, \ldots, m; j = 1, \ldots, n$), is assigned to indicate the degree to which each alternative achieves each attribute. Again the decision maker must first select a scale to use (usually either 0 to 10 or 0 to 100). The worth, ν_j, of the jth alternative is then computed using a linear weighted sum relationship and the alternative with the highest value of ν is selected as the best option.

The main advantage of the scoring methods is in their ease of use. Moreover, scoring methods help the decision maker structure and analyze the decision problem. The greatest disadvantage of these approaches is that they tend to be ad hoc procedures with little theoretical foundation to support them.

II. **Utility-based methods.**   The multiattribute value function (MAV) and multiattribute utility function (MAUT) fall into this category. Value functions are used for deterministic problems while utility functions are used for problems with probabilistic outcomes. In both methods the decision maker usually answers some trade-off questions to specify the single-attribute utility (value) functions, to select the form of the multiattribute function, and to determine the scaling constants.

The primary advantage of these approaches is that the problem becomes a single-objective problem once the utility (value) function has been assessed correctly, thus ensuring achievement of the best-compromise solution. The disadvantages of these methods are: (1) because a single-attribute utility function must be defined for each criterion (attribute), the solution process becomes time consuming as the number of criteria increases; (2) the decision maker must articulate his or her preferences among alternatives that may not have any practical reality (French, 1984); and (3) certain assumptions (for example, mutual preferential independence, mutual utility independence) must be satisfied in order for these methods to apply.

III. Analytic hierarchy process. The analytic hierarchy process (AHP) is a multicriteria decision-making technique that allows the consideration of both objective and subjective factors in selecting the best alternative. This approach is used to arrive at a cardinal ranking of alternatives for multiattribute decision problems.

The analytic hierarchy process is based on three principles: decomposition, comparative judgments, and synthesis of priorities. The *decomposition principle* requires that the decision problem be decomposed into a hierarchy that captures the important elements of the problem. The *principle of comparative judgments* requires that pairwise comparisons (on a scale of relative importance) of elements within a given level with respect to their parent in the next higher level be assessed. These assessments are collected into comparison matrices where each entry in the matrix belongs to the relative importance scale used in the comparisons. The entries in the matrix are then used to generate a derived-ratio scale which reflects the local priorities of the elements in the hierarchy. The *synthesis of priorities principle* takes each of the derived-ratio-scale local priorities in the various levels of the hierarchy and constructs a composite (global) set of priorities for the elements in the lowest level of the hierarchy.

The advantages of AHP are as follows: (1) it allows consideration of both objective and subjective attributes; (2) it provides a means for measuring the consistency of the decision maker's judgments, and, in fact, it is the only approach for solving multiattribute decision problems that has such a capability; and (3) the availability of several software packages for AHP has made it a popular technique. Disadvantages include: (1) rank reversal: the reversal of the preference order of the alternatives when new options are introduced in the problem; (2) the ambiguity in the meaning of the relative importance of one factor when compared to another, and (3) the use of a 1 to 9 scale. In spite of these criticisms, however, AHP remains one of the most widely used multicriteria decision-making approaches.

IV. Goal programming (GP). This approach can be used only when there exists an explicit mathematical relationship between the decision variables and the objectives and constraints. GP is a good technique for identifying an acceptable solution when a minimum acceptable achievement level (goal) has been defined for each objective. Note that for some forms of GP (preemptive GP, for example) a nondominated solution is not guaranteed. GP is a suitable approach for deterministic mathematical programming problems, and, as long as the decision maker is capable of articulating target levels for objectives, the method can accommodate decision problems that include a relatively large number of objectives. The main disadvantages of this approach are the often ad hoc nature of goal selection and the fact that the decision maker is expected to supply information with no knowledge of what the feasible trade-offs in the nondominated set are (the decision maker can, however, learn in the process). It may also be difficult for the decision maker to construct the mathematical relationships.

V. Outranking methods.   These methods are a class of multicriteria decision-making techniques that provide an ordinal ranking (and sometimes only a partial ordering) of the alternatives. One of the original forms of outranking methods is ELECTRE I. Several modifications of the ELECTRE I method (ELECTRE II, III, and the Promethede method) have been developed; we describe only the original approach here.

ELECTRE I allows the decision maker to choose the alternatives that are preferred for most of the criteria and do not result in an unacceptable level of any one criterion. This approach examines the nondominated alternatives and searches for a subset of the nondominated solutions for which a certain degree of dissension is acceptable to the decision maker. Preference relationships between the ith and jth alternatives are established for each criterion; these preference relations are then synthesized for each alternative to produce the outranking relationship. The outranking relationship is used to form a graph in which each node of the graph represents a nondominated alternative, and the graph is used to determine which of the alternatives is preferred. The advantages of this approach include (1) the ability to consider both objective and subjective criteria, and (2) the least amount of information required from the decision maker. Its major disadvantage is that a complete ranking of the alternatives may not be achieved.

5.2.2 Methods Based on the Progressive Articulation of Preferences

Methods within this class are also referred to as interactive methods. These methods solve multiple-objective mathematical programming problems using an iterative process. During this process, the decision maker is presented with information such as a nondominated solution, a set of solutions, or trade-offs among the objectives at the current time. The decision maker then provides local information on his or her preferences among the objectives and/or alternatives. This information allows the formulation of a single-criterion subproblem, which is then solved. The new solution and the outcome are then presented to the decision maker to determine new local information. The process is repeated until the decision maker either converges toward a best-compromise solution or terminates the process prior to reaching that point.

The advantages of these methods are: (1) the decision maker is involved throughout the process, allowing a better understanding of the problem; (2) he or she provides only local information; (3) because the decision maker is involved in the process, he or she may more easily accept the outcome; and (4) less restrictive assumptions are required (as compared to the assumptions required by methods based on the prior articulation of methods). The disadvantages of these methods are: (1) the interaction process with the decision maker may be time-consuming, (2) there are generally no software packages available for these methods, and (3) there is no guarantee that the best-compromise solution will be obtained within a finite number of cycles.

I. Interactive surrogate worth trade-off method (ISWT).   This method consists of two phases. In the first step the decision maker chooses a primary objective and provides reasonable values for the right-hand side of the remaining objectives treated as constraints. Then a nondominated solution is generated using the constraint approach and pairwise trade-offs between the primary objective and each of the other objectives are determined at the nondominated solution point, after which the decision maker provides worth values for each of the trade-offs (on a scale of -10 to $+10$). If the decision maker is satisfied with the solution the process stops. Otherwise, the worth values are used to generate new values for the right-hand sides of the objectives and the process is repeated.

The advantages of this approach include: (1) only pairwise comparisons are made during the assessment of the worth function, and (2) it can support both linear and nonlinear models. The disadvantages of the approach are: (1) as the number of objectives increase, there is an excessive demand on the decision maker to identify the worth function, and (2) the attainment of the best-compromise solution is not guaranteed.

II. STEM.   STEM starts with maximizing (or minimizing) each of the objectives separately and constructs a $p \times p$ payoff matrix (where p is the number of objectives). (Note that the solutions in this table are all nondominated solutions.) The diagonal elements of the matrix give an outcome associated with an ideal solution. Unfortunately, due to the conflicting nature of the objectives, an ideal solution usually does not exist. However, the ideal solution provides a standard by which the nondominated solutions can be evaluated. The next step involves identifying the nondominated solution with the least deviation from the ideal solution. The decision maker is then asked to identify the satisfactory and unsatisfactory objectives and specify the amount by which the satisfactory objectives can be decreased in order to improve the level of unsatisfactory objectives. The lower bounds on the satisfactory objectives are added as constraints to the original problem and the revised problem is solved to identify a new solution for the next iteration. This process continues until the decision maker is satisfied with a solution.

The advantages of STEM include (1) the minimal burden on the decision maker, (2) the learning gained by the decision maker during the process, and (3) application to integer and nonlinear multiobjective programs of any size that can be solved by single-objective optimization software. The main disadvantage of this method is that the decision maker cannot make a clear choice of which objective to relax or by how much.

III. Geoffrion-Dyer-Feinberg (GDF).
GDF is a search procedure that, through interactions with the decision maker at each step, moves toward improved feasible solutions. The method begins with a nondominated solution and determines the direction of greatest improvement. To estimate the direction, the decision maker answers pairwise comparison questions to provide a trade-off ratio between objective f_i and the reference objective f_1. Once the direction of improvement is established, the decision maker is again solicited to provide information regarding the step length to be taken in this direction. The search is terminated when the decision maker is satisfied with a solution or when the improvement between two steps is less than some specified value.

Because of the type of information required in this approach (that is, pairwise comparisons and stepwise responses), GDF places a considerable burden on the decision maker. Moreover, the difficulty of estimating the marginal rates of substitution (trade-off ratio between objective f_i and the reference objective f_1) may cause poor convergence to the best-compromise solution. Therefore, GDF is not an easy approach for users to understand and use.

IV. Zionts and Wallenius method.
This method uses linear approximations of the objective functions and constraints and assumes that the implicit utility function is a linear function of the original objective functions. To start the method, a linear composite function of the original objectives is constructed using a set of arbitrarily chosen positive weights that sum to 1. The resulting single-objective problem is solved using linear programming to produce a nondominated solution. Because this nondominated extreme point may not be the best-compromise solution, adjacent nondominated extreme points are presented to the decision maker for consideration. The trade-offs for each of the nondominated solutions are presented to the decision maker, who then decides whether the trade-offs are desirable, undesirable, or neither. Based on this information, a new set of weights is constructed and a new composite objective function is generated. The resulting single-objective problem is solved using linear programming and a nondominated extreme point is identified. The process is repeated until the decision maker is satisfied with the solution.

One advantage of this approach is that the Z-W algorithm can converge quickly to local preferable solutions. In addition, it places less of a burden on the decision maker than the GDF and the ISWT. The major disadvantage of this approach is that for large problems a large number of nonbasic variables must be considered, which makes the approach infeasible to use. Moreover, the assumption-of-linear-utility model is not always practical in real life.

V. Tchebycheff approach.
Similar to STEM, the Tchebycheff approach begins with the generation of the ideal point, which represents the best value of each objective function. A large sample of nondominated solutions are then generated through the use of the weighting method (described in Chapter 3) and are presented to the decision maker. This set is then filtered to a reasonable number of nondominated solutions to be presented to the decision maker through two processes. The first filtering process

involves selecting a subset of the original set containing solutions that are most different in terms of the values of the decision variables. From this subset, the ideal point is used in a second filtering process to select those solutions that are most different in terms of the objective function values. This two-step process ensures that the remaining set includes a manageable number of nondominated solutions and that the solutions represent the entire decision and objective space. The decision maker then selects a most preferred solution from this set. If satisfied with this solution, the decision maker terminates the search; otherwise he or she computes ranges for each of the elements in the weighting vector by using the ideal point and the current preferred solution. New nondominated solutions are again generated by randomly selecting weights within the specified ranges. This process continues until the decision maker is satisfied with a solution.

The advantages of this approach are: (1) because the decision maker selects only the most preferred solution, the burden on him or her is reduced, and (2) a small number of solutions are presented to the decision maker in each iteration. A disadvantage of this method is its sensitivity to the starting conditions: The original sample of nondominated solutions that are generated at the beginning of the method can have a large impact on the final outcome.

VI. Interactive and visual interactive goal programming.   This approach is similar to the goal programming described above except that, after the solution is obtained, the decision maker is asked to make any desired changes to the goal types, target values, and penalty weights. The new problem is then solved to generate the next iteration process. Interactive GP is an unstructured approach for exploring the feasible region and requires a great deal of intuition on the part of the decision maker. An advantage of this technique is that several software packages are available, some of which show results graphically (see, for example, VIG™,* developed by Korhonen and Laakso, 1986). A major disadvantage of this approach is that a nondominated solution is not guaranteed.

5.2.3 Methods Based on the Posterior Articulation of Preferences

The techniques that rely on posterior articulation of preferences are the least commonly used of the three classes of multicriteria approaches. The majority of the methods in this category are applied to multiple-objective mathematical programming problems. These methods first try to find all or almost all of the nondominated solutions to the problem. The nondominated solutions are then presented to the decision maker to select the preferred one through elicitation of preference information. Because multiple-objective problems usually have an infinite number of nondominated solutions, choosing a single preferred solution can be very cumbersome. Note, however,

---

*VIG™ is marketed by NumPlan Ltd., P.O. Box 128, 03101 Nummela, Finland.

that there are techniques available for reducing a large set of nondominated solutions to a manageable number.

As with the interactive methods, posterior methods generally require the generation of nondominated solutions through either the weighting or the constraint approach. The decision maker is then required to provide one of several types of information regarding the nondominated solutions (for example, preferences among the nondominated solutions or preferences for trade-offs between the objectives). In most cases the information required by a posterior method is more cumbersome to obtain than that required by progressive methods because of the size of the set of nondominated solutions. However, the information is only elicited once.

In Chapter 4, we elected to describe only one of these approaches—data envelopment analysis. Its advantages and disadvantages are briefly described below.

DEA.   Data envelopment analysis is a methodology used to analyze the relative efficiency of each of several alternatives (referred to as decision making units). The basic elements of a DEA analysis are the decision making units (DMUs), inputs (where less is better), and outputs (where more is better). The viewpoint taken is that an increase in an input is expected to yield an increase in an output. However, the viewpoint is also that it is desirable to minimize inputs because the inputs require resources and thus result in a cost.

DEA analysis provides several useful results. It constructs the so-called envelopment surface (also called a production function or efficient frontier). This allows one to determine which of the DMUs (alternatives) are efficient and which are inefficient. The production function shows the maximum amount of outputs that can be achieved by combining various inputs. Alternatively, it shows the minimum amount of inputs required to achieve a given output level.

DEA analysis also establishes an inefficiency metric. The inefficiency metric allows one to evaluate other DMUs (alternatives) based on their distance to the envelopment surface (frontier). DEA analysis can identify the sources and degrees of the inefficiencies.

DEA has been applied in a large number of applications. Its advantages are: (1) it does not require information from the decision maker, and (2) existing LP and NLP software may be used to analyze the alternatives. Its major disadvantages are: (1) the formulations of the optimization problems can be difficult for the user to understand, and (2) DEA does not explicitly rank the alternatives.

5.3 A Guide for Selecting an MCDM Technique

Because of the choice from among a large number of available multiple-criteria decision-making (MCDM) methods, the user actually faces a multiple-criteria problem when trying to select a method. It may be a difficult task to identify the most suitable method for a given situation because different decision problems have distinct characteristics. Moreover, the decision makers, who must provide the preference information, differ in their decision-making styles and preferences. The selection problem is an important one because experiments have shown that the alternative that is selected as "best" can depend on the choice of methods and even on such irrelevant factors as the questioning technique (see Hobbs, 1986). In other words, even if the problem has been structured perfectly, the use of an inappropriate method can lead to decisions that cannot be justified (Ozernoy, 1992). The purpose of this section is to provide a set of guidelines for selecting an appropriate MCDM method for given a decision problem.

There are several factors that should be considered when selecting an MCDM solution method. We classify these factors as: (1) characteristics of the decision problem, (2) characteristics of the decision maker, and (3) characteristics of the solution technique.

Characteristics of the decision problem include (a) the size and complexity of the problem, which we define as the number of objectives, criteria, alternatives, and constraints, and (b) the amount of uncertainty present in the problem, that is, the degree of risk and uncertainty in the nature of the relationship between elements and consequences of decisions.

Characteristics of the decision maker include the ability and/or desire of the decision maker to articulate various amounts and types of preference information (Evans, 1984). Note that all MCDM techniques assume that the decision maker is capable of supplying preference information either implicitly or explicitly. Depending on how explicit this preference information is, either the decision maker is capable of articulating a stable preference structure prior to solution or does not have a stable preference structure prior to solution and is capable of identifying preferences only during the process.

Characteristics of the solution technique include (a) ease of use defined in terms of amount of cognitive burden it places on the decision maker, computer code availability, and learning curve; (b) total time required to solve the problem, including solution time and interaction time with the decision maker; (c) accuracy, defined in terms of whether the technique guarantees a nondominated solution and whether it converges to the theoretical optimal solution of the problem with respect to the decision makers preference structure; and (d) restrictiveness of the underlying assumptions.

In order to select an appropriate technique, the characteristics of the decision problem and the decision maker must be studied against the characteristics of the solution technique so that the best match can be identified. Table 5.2 provides a summary that includes an evaluation of each technique described in this book with respect to the characteristics of the decision problem, decision maker, and the solution technique, as discussed above.

We conclude this chapter with several papers that provide further discussions and comparisons of multiple-criteria methods. These comparisons of methods, used in practice, can provide the reader with useful insight into the appropriate choice of method.

Table 5.2 Criteria for Selecting Multiple-Criteria Decision-Making Techniques

MCDM methods	Type of DM information required	Ease of Use			Time and Effort		Accuracy	Assumptions
		Software availability	Learning curve	Cognitive burden	DM interaction	Time to solution		
Scoring Methods	Scores on attributes and objectives	None, (but easy to develop)	Low	Low	Moderate, increases with problem size	DM time: moderate; solution time: low	DM preference structure not captured	Nonrestrictive
Multiattribute Value Function	Weights and value functions on attributes	Available	Moderate	High	High, increases with problem size	DM time: moderate; solution time: low	DM preference structure is captured	Very restrictive
Multiattribute Utility Function	Weights and utility functions on attributes using lotteries	Available	High	High	High, increases with problem size	DM time: high; solution time: low	DM preference structure is captured	Very restrictive
Analytic Hierarchy Process	Pairwise comparisons of attributes and alternatives	Available	Low	Low to moderate	High, increases with problem size	DM time: moderate; solution time: low	DM preference structure is captured	Moderately restrictive
ELECTRE I, II, III	Rating scale for criteria weights and discordance index	None (but easy to develop)	Low	Low	Moderate, increases with problem size	DM time: moderate; solution time: low	DM preference structure is captured as a partial ordering	Nonrestrictive
Goal Programming	Priorities or aspiration levels on goals	Available	Low	Low to moderate	Small, increases with problem size	DM time: low; setup time: high; solution time: low	Nondominated solution not guaranteed	Nonrestrictive
Data Envelopment Analysis	No DM preferences are used	None*	N/A†	N/A†	N/A†	Setup time: high; solution time: moderate	Nondominated solution is guaranteed	Nonrestrictive

Method	Input required from DM	Software available†			Computational effort	DM, setup, and solution time	Generation of nondominated solutions	Restrictions on problem type
Interactive Surrogate Worth Trade-off Method	Limits on objectives and worth values on trade-offs	None*	Low	Low to moderate	Moderate, increases with problem size	DM time: moderate; setup time: high; solution time: moderate	Nondominated solution is guaranteed	Nonrestrictive
STEP	Degree of satisfaction of objectives	None*	Low	Low	Moderate, increases with problem size	DM time: moderate; setup time: high; solution time: moderate	Nondominated solution is guaranteed	Nonrestrictive
GDF	Trade-off between objectives and solution preferences	None*	Moderate	Moderate	Moderate to high, increases with problem size	DM time: moderate; setup time: high; solution time: moderate	Nondominated solution is guaranteed	Nonrestrictive
Zionts and Wallenius	Desirability of trade-offs	None*	Low	Low to moderate	Moderate, increases with problem size	DM time: low; setup time: high; solution time: moderate	Nondominated solution is guaranteed	Nonrestrictive
Tchebycheff	Selection of most preferred solution and ranges of weights on the objectives	None*	Moderate	Moderate	Moderate, increases with problem size	DM time: moderate; setup time: high; solution time: moderate	Nondominated solution is guaranteed	Nonrestrictive
Interactive Goal Programming	Priorities on goals, penalty weights	None*	Low	Low to moderate	Moderate, increases with problem size	DM time: moderate; setup time: moderate; solution time: moderate	Nondominated solution is not guaranteed	Nonrestrictive

*Although no specific commercially available software is available for these methods, the subproblems can easily be solved using any LP or NLP solver such as GINO, LINDO, the problem solver in EXCEL, or CPLEX.

†DEA analyzes the efficiency of a set of alternatives. It does not determine the most preferred solution and does not require input from the decision maker.

Annotated Bibliography

Bard, J., "A Comparison of the Analytic Hierarchy Process with Multiattribute Utility Theory: A Case Study," *IIE Trans.*, Vol. 24, No. 5, 1992, pp. 111–121.

Summary: This paper describes the real world experience of using the analytic hierarchy process and multiattribute utility theory for selecting the next generation of rough terrain cargo handlers for the US Army. The author found that the AHP was more accessible and conducive to consensus building. The MAUT analysis was found to be time-consuming and frustrating for users.

Belton, V., "A Comparison of the Analytic Hierarchy Process and a Simple Multi-Attribute Value Function," *European J. Operational Research*, Vol. 26, 1986, pp. 7–21.

Summary: Belton provides a comparison of the analytic hierarchy process and simple multiattribute value function approaches to find the best alternative from a short-list of options and a large number of attributes. The methods are compared from both theoretical and practical standpoints. The author discusses the practical implications of the use of each approach.

Buchanan, J.T., and H.G. Daellenbach, "A Comparative Evaluation of Interactive Solution Methods for Multiple Objective Decision Models," *European J. Operational Research*, Vol. 29, 1987, pp. 353–359.

Summary: This paper describes an experiment used to compare four of the interactive methods. The methods were compared in terms of their performance from the users point of view. The authors indicate that the decision-making characteristics of the user have a direct impact on the perceived performance of the methods.

French, S., "Interactive Multi-Objective Programming: Its Aims, Applications and Demands," *J. Operational Research Soc.*, Vol. 35, No. 9, 1984, pp. 827–834.

Summary: The author provides a critical review of the interactive multiple-objective programming methods and discusses how these methods may not be valid because their underlying assumptions are not supported by empirical results of behavioral decision theory.

Hobbs, B.F., "What Can We Learn from Experiments in Multiobjective Decision Analysis?" *IEEE Trans. Systems, Man, and Cybernetics*, Vol. 16, No. 3, 1986, pp. 384–394.

Summary: This study provides an overview of factors that affect the choice and use of existing multiobjective methods (for example, purpose of method, ease of use, validity, form of output). The author suggests that the use of multiple techniques on the same problem can help clarify the differences among the methods.

Klein, G., Moskowitz, H., and A. Ravindran, "Comparative Evaluation of Prior Versus Progressive Articulation of Preference in Bicriterion Optimization," *Naval Research Logistics Quarterly*, Vol. 33, 1986, pp. 309–323.

Summary: This paper compares a prior method versus a progressive method for solving a quality control decision problem. The two methods are compared on the basis of ease of use, preferences of the solutions obtained, and insight is provided into the nature and structure of the problem. The authors demonstrate that each method has advantages and disadvantages, and suggest that a hybrid approach may be appropriate.

Min, H., and J. Storbeck, "On the Origin and Persistence of Misconception in Goal Programming," *J. Operational Research Soc.*, Vol. 42, No. 4, 1991, pp. 301–312.

Summary: The authors provide a balanced discussion of the pros and cons of goal programming, stating that the efficiency of goal programming solutions is problem-dependent and user-dependent; consequently, goal programming can be misused. The resultant warning is that if unreasonable targets are set for the goals, then goal programming will not provide the best available or efficient solution.

Olson, D.L., "Review of Empirical Studies in Multiobjective Mathematical Programming: Subject Reflection of Nonlinear Utility and Learning," *Decision Sciences*, Vol. 23, 1992, pp. 1–23.

Summary: This paper reviews a number of published studies where human subjects were used to test a number of features of multiple-objective programming methods. The author finds that a number of useful tools have been developed to aid real decision making under conditions of complex trade-offs. He recommends that there is a need to better understand effective human decision making and that the focus of the methods be redirected to effectively aid human learning and to support group decisions.

References

Evans, G.W., "An Overview of Techniques for Solving Multiobjective Mathematical Programs," *Management Science*, Vol. 30, No. 11, 1984, pp. 1268–1282.

French, S., "Interactive Multiobjective Programming: Its Aims, Applications, and Demands," *J. Operational Research Soc.*, Vol. 35, No. 9, 1984, pp. 827–834.

Hobbs, B.F., "What Can We Learn from Experiments in Multiobjective Decision Analysis?" *IEEE Trans. Systems, Man, and Cybernetics*, Vol. 16, No. 3, 1986, pp. 384–394.

Korhonen, P., and J. Laakso, "A Visual Interactive Method for Solving the Multiple Criteria Problem," *European J. Operational Research*, Vol. 24, 1986, pp. 277–287.

Ozernoy, V., "Choosing the Best Multiple Criteria Decision-Making Method," *INFOR*, Vol. 30, No. 2, 1992, pp. 159–171.

The Authors

Mansooreh Mollaghasemi is an Associate Professor in the Department of Industrial Engineering and Management Systems at the University of Central Florida. Her current research interests are in the area of multiple-criteria decision making, simulation modeling and analysis of complex systems, and multiple-response simulation optimization.

Julia Pet-Edwards is an Assistant Professor in the Department of Industrial Engineering and Management Systems at the University of Central Florida. Her current research interests are in the area of multiple-criteria decision making, with a particular emphasis in risk management of extreme events.